Mountain Biking
Denver and Boulder

SECOND EDITION

BOB D'ANTONIO

FALCON GUIDES ®

GUILFORD, CONNECTICUT
HELENA, MONTANA

AN IMPRINT OF THE GLOBE PEQUOT PRESS

Maps created by Sue Cary © Morris Book Publishing, LLC

ISBN 978-0-7627-2467-3
ISSN 1540-8701

Manufactured in the United States of America
Second Edition/Fourth

To buy books in quantity for corporate use
or incentives, call **(800) 962–0973**
or e-mail **premiums@GlobePequot.com.**

Contents

The Rides

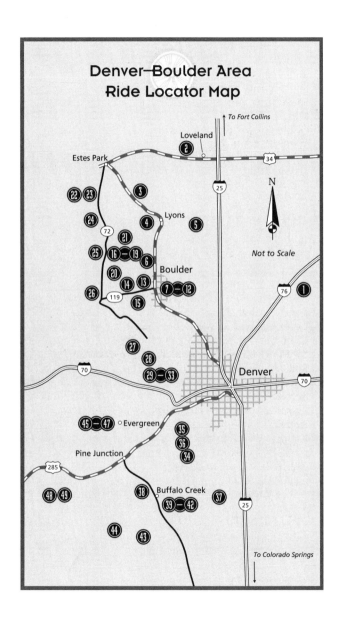

Denver–Boulder Area
Ride Locator Map

Legend

Interstate	🛡55	City	▦
U.S. Highway	🛡50	Town	○
State Highway/ County Road	(135)	Campground	▲
Cliff		Structures	■
Interstate		Mountain/Peak	▲
U.S. Highway		Trailhead	🅣
Paved Road		Parking Area	🅟
Maintained Dirt		Overview	◻
Unmaintained Dirt/ Doubletrack		Picnic Area	🚻
Singletrack Trail		Gate	•—•
Selected Route		Property Boundary	⌐_⌐
Waterway		Map Orientation	N ↑
Lake/Reservoir			
Spring	○—	Scale	0 — Miles — 6

Dedication

This book is dedicated to my nephew Justin Alf, who loved the trails on the Front Range and will be sorely missed on our rides and in our lives. All of your family and friends miss you.

Acknowledgments

Thanks to all the fine folks who purchased the first edition of this book. Thanks to my family for all of their support with this and all my outdoor projects. Thanks to all the land managers, volunteers, IMBA, and anyone who supports the sport of mountain biking in the Denver/Boulder area. Also a heartfelt thanks to John at Dean Bicycles for building the best bikes around.

Get Ready to Crank!

Where to ride? It's a quandary that faces every mountain biker, beginner or expert, local or expatriate.

If you're new to the area, where do you start? If you're a long-time local, how do you avoid the rut of riding the same old trails week after week? And how do you find new terrain that's challenging but not overwhelming? Or an easier ride for when your not-so-serious buddies want to come along?

Welcome to *Mountain Biking Denver and Boulder,* second edition. Here are forty-nine rides ranging from easy road routes to smooth singletrack to bravado-busting boulder fields. The rides are described in plain language, with accurate distances and ratings for physical and technical difficulty. Each entry offers a wealth of detailed information that's easy to read and use, from an armchair or on the trail.

Our aim here is three-fold: to help you choose a ride that's appropriate for your fitness and skill level; to make it easy to find the trailhead; and to help you complete the ride safely, without getting lost. Take care of these basics, and fun is bound to break loose.

The Denver–Boulder Backcountry: What to Expect

The rides in this book cover a wide variety of terrains. Many of the rides are mountainous, and that means two things: They are steep and rough, and weather can be unpredictable—at times severe.

Mountain terrain requires preparedness. Get in good shape before you attempt any of these rides, and know your limits. Keep your bike running smoothly with frequent cleaning and maintenance. Do a quick check before each ride to ensure that tires, rims, brakes, handlebars, seat, shifters, derailleurs, and chain all survived the last ride intact and are functioning properly.

Always carry at least one water bottle (and don't forget to fill it). A snack, such as fruit or sports energy bars, will help keep those mighty thighs cranking for many hours. Dress for the weather and pack a wind- and waterproof jacket whenever there's any doubt. Don't forget sunglasses, sunscreen, lip balm, and insect repellent, as needed.

I tend to go light on tools, but a pump and tube patch kit can save you from a long walk or, on longer rides, a night out. It also helps to carry one or two Allen wrenches for tightening or adjusting seat posts, handlebars, chainrings, pedals, brake posts, and other components. Some folks aren't comfortable unless they bring twenty pounds of tools; you can usually hear them coming, but they rarely get stranded by mechanical problems.

This book is designed to be easily carried along in a jersey pocket or bike bag, and the maps and ride descriptions will help anyone unfamiliar with the trails. For a more detailed picture of the terrain (ride routes are not always shown) scan a county open-space map or national forest map beforehand. The correct maps are listed in the at-a-glance information for each ride.

Cycling gloves are another essential piece of safety equipment—saving hands from cuts and bruises because of falls or encroaching branches and rocks. They also improve your grip and comfort on the handlebars. Finally, always wear a helmet; it can save your life.

Weather along the Front Range spans the gamut of North American extremes, sometimes in one twenty-four-hour period. Snow can fall any day of the year, but summer highs may top 100 degrees Fahrenheit. In general, higher elevations are cooler (by as much as 10 degrees Fahrenheit for every 1,000 feet gained) and windier. If you are driving to a trailhead, play it safe and take a variety of clothes in the car to match the variable weather you may encounter.

Most of the good off-road riding in the greater Denver area happens from mid-March through October. Some trails, particularly at higher elevations, have shorter seasons running from late May through September. (Bear in mind that hunting seasons in some areas may overlap prime pedaling times. For specific dates, check with the Colorado Division of Wildlife (see Appendix).

At any time of year, rain or snow can turn trails to gumbo for days afterward. Please stay off wet, muddy trails. The risk of soil damage and erosion is simply too great. In general, the valley rides and lower trails in the Denver area open and dry out earlier than other area trails. Be aware, however, that heavy runoff may make some stream crossings unsafe, even when the adjoining trails are dry and passable.

It is possible to ride year-round in the Denver area. Most trails closer to town stay open in drier years: Try Meyers Homestead Trail (Ride 8), Flagstaff Road (Ride 9), Foothills Trail/Boulder Valley Ranch Trail (Ride 10), Marshall Mesa/Community Ditch Trail (Ride 11), Teller Lake

(Ride 12), Green Mountain Park Loop (Ride 29), and Dakota Ridge and Matthew/Winters Park Loop (Ride 30).

Rules of the Trail

Rules? I can almost hear the groans of mountain bikers all too accustomed to finding NO BIKES signs or lists of dos and don'ts at every trailhead.

Of course, if every mountain biker always yielded the right-of-way, stayed on the trail, avoided wet or muddy trails, never cut switchbacks, never skidded, always rode in control, showed respect for other trail users, and carried out every last scrap of what was carried in (candy wrappers and bike-part debris included)—in short, *did the right thing*—then we wouldn't need a list of rules governing our behavior. Fact is, most mountain bikers *are* conscientious and are trying to do the right thing. Most of us *own* that integrity. (No one becomes good at something as demanding and painful as grunting up sheer mountainsides by cheating.)

Most of us don't need rules.

But we do need knowledge. What exactly *is* the right thing to do?

Here are some guidelines—I like to think of them as reminders—reprinted by permission of the International Mountain Bicycling Association (IMBA). The basic theme here is to reduce or eliminate any damage to the land and water, the plant and wildlife inhabitants, and other backcountry visitors and trail users. Ride with respect.

IMBA Rules of the Trail

Thousands of miles of dirt trails have been closed to mountain bicyclists. The irresponsible riding habits of a few riders have been a factor. Do your part to maintain trail access by observing the following rules of the trail, formulated by IMBA, whose mission is to promote environmentally sound and socially responsible mountain biking.

1. Ride on open trails only. Respect trail and road closures (ask if not sure), avoid possible trespass on private land, and obtain permits and authorization as may be required. Federal and state wilderness areas are closed to cycling. The way you ride will influence trail management decisions and policies.

2. Leave no trace. Be sensitive to the dirt beneath you. Even on open (legal) trails, you should not ride under conditions where you will leave evidence of your passing, such as on certain soils after a rain. Recognize different types of soil and trail construction; practice low-impact cycling. This also means staying on existing trails and not creating any new ones. Be sure to pack out at least as much as you pack in.

3. Control your bicycle! Inattention for even a second can cause problems. Obey all bicycle speed regulations and recommendations.

4. Always yield trail. Make known your approach well in advance. A friendly greeting (or bell) is considerate and works well; don't startle others. Show your respect when passing by slowing to a walking pace or even stopping.

Anticipate other trail users around corners or in blind spots.

5. Never spook animals. An unannounced approach, a sudden movement, or a loud noise startles all animals. This can be dangerous for you, others, and the animals. Give animals extra room and time to adjust to you. When passing horses use special care and follow directions from the horseback riders (ask if uncertain). Running cattle and disturbing wildlife is a serious offense. Leave gates as you found them, or as marked.

6. Plan ahead. Know your equipment, your ability, and the area in which you are riding—and prepare accordingly. Be self-sufficient at all times, keep your equipment in good repair, and carry necessary supplies for changes in weather or other conditions. A well-executed trip is a satisfaction to you and not a burden or offense to others. Always wear a helmet.

Keep trails open by setting a good example of environmentally sound and socially responsible off-road cycling.

How to Use This Guide

Mountain Biking Denver and Boulder describes forty-nine mountain bike rides in their entirety.

Twenty-eight of the featured rides are loops, beginning and ending at the same point but coming and going on different trails. Loops are by far the most popular type of ride, and Front Range riders are lucky to have so many so close to home.

Be forewarned, however: The difficulty of a loop ride may change dramatically depending on which direction you ride around the loop. If you are unfamiliar with the rides in this book, try them first as described here. The directions follow the path of least resistance (which does not necessarily mean "easy"). After you've been over the terrain, you can determine whether a given loop would be fun—or even feasible—in the reverse direction.

Portions of some rides follow gravel and even paved roads, and one ride never wanders off road. Purists may wince at road rides in a book about mountain biking, but these are special rides. They offer a chance to enjoy the mountain scenery and fresh air while covering easier, non-technical terrain for people new to the sport. Hard-core riders can also use them on "active rest" days or when mud or snow close higher-elevation trails.

Each ride description in this book follows the same format:

Number and name of the ride: Rides are cross-referenced by number throughout this book. In many cases, parts of rides or entire routes can be linked to other rides for longer trips or variations on a standard route. These opportunities are noted, followed by "see Ride(s) #."

For the names of rides, I relied on official names of trails, roads, and natural features as shown on national forest and U.S. Geological Survey maps. In some cases, deference was given to long-term local custom.

Location: The general whereabouts of the ride and directions from Denver or Boulder.

Distance: The length of the ride in miles, given as a loop, one way, or round-trip (out and back).

Time: An estimate of how long it takes to complete the ride, for example: 1 to 2 hours. *The time listed is the actual* *riding time and does not include rest stops.* Strong, skilled riders may be able to do a given ride in less than the estimated time, while other riders may take considerably longer. Also bear in mind that severe weather, changes in trail conditions, or mechanical problems may prolong a ride.

Tread: The type of road or trail: paved road, gravel road, dirt road or four-wheel-drive track, doubletrack, ATV-width singletrack, and singletrack.

Aerobic level: The level of physical effort required to complete the ride: easy, moderate, or strenuous. (See the explanation of the rating system under Aerobic Level Ratings).

Technical difficulty: The level of bike-handling skills needed to complete the ride upright and in one piece. Technical difficulty is rated on a scale from 1 to 5, with 1 being the easiest and 5 the hardest. (See the explanation of the rating system under Technical Difficulty Ratings).

Hazards: A list of dangers that may be encountered on a ride, including traffic, weather, trail obstacles and conditions, risky stream crossings, difficult route-finding, and other perils. Remember: Conditions may change at any time. Be alert for storms, new fences, downfall, missing trail signs, and mechanical failure. Fatigue, heat, cold, and/or dehydration may impair judgment. Always wear a helmet and other safety equipment. Ride in control at all times.

Highlights: Special features or qualities that make a ride worth doing (as if we needed an excuse!): scenery, fun singletrack, chances to see wildlife.

Land status: A list of managing agencies or land owners. Most of the rides in this book are on national forest or county open space. But many of the rides also cross portions of private, state, or municipal lands. Always leave gates as you found them. And respect the land, regardless of who owns it. See the Appendix for a list of local addresses for land-managing agencies.

Maps: A list of available maps. Not all routes are shown on official maps.

Access: How to find the trailhead or the start of the ride. A number of rides can be pedaled right from town; for others it's best to drive to the trailhead.

The Ride: A mile-by-mile list of key points—landmarks, notable climbs and descents, stream crossings, obstacles, hazards, major turns, and junctions—along the ride. All distances were measured to the tenth of a mile with a cyclo-computer (a bike-mounted odometer). Terrain, riding technique, and even tire pressure can affect odometer readings, so treat all mileage as estimates.

Finally, one last reminder that the real world is changing all the time. The information presented here is as accurate and up-to-date as possible, but there are no guarantees out in the mountains. You alone are responsible for your safety and for the choices you make on the trail.

If you do find an error or omission in this book, or a new and noteworthy change in the field, I'd like to hear from you. Contact me at The Globe Pequot Press, Reader Response/Editorial Department, P.O. Box 480 Guilford, CT 06437.

Elevation Graphs

An elevation profile accompanies each ride description. Here the ups and downs of the route are graphed on a grid of elevation (in feet above sea level) on the left; and miles pedaled, across the top. Route surface conditions (see map legend) and technical levels are shown on the graphs.

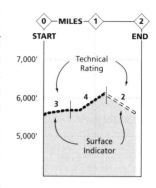

Note that these graphs are compressed (squeezed) to fit on the page. The actual slopes you will ride are not as steep as the lines drawn on the graphs (it just feels that way). In addition, some extremely short dips and climbs are too small to show up on the graphs. All such abrupt changes in gradient are, however, mentioned in the mile-by-mile ride description.

Rating the Rides

One of the first lessons learned by most mountain bikers is to not trust their friends' accounts of how easy or difficult a given ride may be.

"Where ya wanna' ride today?"

"Let's do 'The Wall,' dudes—it's gnarly in the middle, but even my grandma could fly up that last hill, and the view is way cool."

If you don't read between the lines, only painful experience will tell you that granny won the pro-elite class in last weekend's hillclimb race and "the view" is over the handlebars from the lip of a 1,000-foot drop on that fun little gnarly stretch.

So how do you know what you're getting into before it's too late?

Don't always listen to your friends.

But do read this book. Falcon Guides rate each ride for two types of difficulty: the *physical effort* required to pedal the distance and the level of *bike-handling skills* needed to stay upright and make it home in one piece. We call these Aerobic level and Technical difficulty.

The following sections explain what the various ratings mean in plain, specific language. An elevation profile accompanies each ride description to help you determine how easy or hard the ride is. Also weigh other factors such as elevation above sea level, total trip distance, weather and wind, and current trail conditions.

Aerobic Level Ratings

Bicycling is often touted as a relaxing, low-impact, relatively easy way to burn excess calories and maintain a healthy heart and lungs. Mountain biking, however, tends to pack a little more work (and excitement) into the routine.

Fat tires and soft or rough trails increase the rolling resistance, so it takes more effort to push those wheels around. And unpaved or off-road hills tend to be steeper than grades measured and tarred by the highway department. When we use the word *steep,* we mean a sweat-inducing, oxygen-sucking, lactose-building climb. If it's followed by an exclamation point—steep (!)—expect some honest pain on the way up (and maybe for days afterward).

So, expect to breathe hard and sweat some, probably a lot. Pedaling around town is a good start, but it won't fully prepare you for the workout offered by most of the rides in this book. If you're unsure of your fitness level, see a doctor for a physical exam before tackling any of the rides in this book. Moreover, if you're riding to get back in shape or just for the fun of it, take it easy. Walk or rest if need be. Start with short rides and add on miles gradually.

Here's how we rate the exertion (aerobic) level for terrain covered in this book:

Easy: Flat or gently rolling terrain. No steeps or prolonged climbs.

Moderate: Some hills. Climbs may be short and fairly steep or long and gradual.

Strenuous: Frequent or prolonged climbs steep enough to require riding in the lowest gear; requires a high level of aerobic fitness, power, and endurance (typically acquired through many hours of riding and proper training). Less fit riders may need to walk.

Many rides are mostly easy and moderate but may have short strenuous sections. Other rides are mostly strenuous and should be attempted only after a complete medical checkup and implant of a second heart, preferably a *big* one. Also, be aware that flailing through a highly technical section can be exhausting even on the flats. Good riding skills and a relaxed stance on the bike save energy.

Finally, any ride can be strenuous if you ride it hard and fast. Conversely, the pain of a lung-burning climb grows easier to tolerate as your fitness level improves. Learn to pace yourself and remember to schedule easy rides and rest days into your calendar.

Technical Difficulty Ratings

While you're pushing up that steep, strenuous slope, wondering how much farther you can go before your lungs prolapse and billow out of your mouth like an air bag in a desperate gasp for oxygen, remember that the dry heaves aren't the only hurdle on the way to the top of the mountain.

There's that tree across the trail, or the sideslope full of ball-bearing-sized pebbles, or the place where the trail disappears except for faint bits of rubber clinging to the smooth, sheer wall of granite straight ahead.

Mountain bikes will roll over or through an amazing array of life's little challenges, but sometimes we, as riders, have to help. Or at least close our eyes and hang on. As a last resort, some riders get off their bikes and walk—get this—*before* they flip over the handlebars. These folks have no sense of adventure. The rest of us hop onto our bikes with only the dimmest inkling of what lies ahead. And later we brag about the ride to hell (leaving out the part about carrying our bikes half the distance because hell has some highly technical terrain).

No more. The technical difficulty ratings in this book help take the worst surprises out of backcountry rides. In the privacy of your own home you can make an honest appraisal of your bike-handling skills and then find rides in these pages that are within your ability.

Technical difficulty is rated on a scale from 1 to 5, from easiest to most difficult. We tried to make the ratings as objective as possible by considering the type of obstacles and their frequency of occurrence. The same standards were applied consistently through all the rides in this book.

We've also added plus (+) and minus (-) symbols to cover gray areas between given levels of difficulty: A 4+ obstacle is harder than a 4, but easier than a 5-. A stretch of trail rated 5+ would be unrideable by all but the most skilled (or luckiest) riders.

Here are the five levels defined:

Level 1: Smooth tread; road or doubletrack; no obstacles, ruts, or steeps. Requires basic bike-riding skills.

Level 2: Mostly smooth tread; wide, well-groomed single-track or road/doubletrack with minor ruts or loose gravel or sand.

Level 3: Irregular tread with some rough sections; single or doubletrack with obvious route choices; some steep sections; occasional obstacles may include small rocks, roots, water bars, ruts, loose gravel or sand, and sharp turns or broad, open switchbacks.

Level 4: Rough tread with few smooth places; singletrack or rough doubletrack with limited route choices; steep sections, some with obstacles; obstacles are numerous and varied, including rocks, roots, branches, ruts, sidehills, narrow tread, loose gravel or sand, and switchbacks.

Level 5: Continuously broken, rocky, root-infested, or trenched tread; singletrack or extremely rough doubletrack with few route choices; frequent, sudden, and severe changes in gradient; some slopes so steep that wheels lift off the ground; obstacles are nearly continuous and may include boulders, logs, water, large holes, deep ruts, ledges, piles of loose gravel, steep sidehills, encroaching trees, and tight switchbacks.

Again, most of the rides in this book cover varied terrain, with an ever-changing degree of technical difficulty. Some trails run smooth with only occasional obstacles, and other trails are seemingly all obstacle. The path of least resistance, or *line,* is where you find it. In general, most obstacles are more challenging if you encounter them while climbing rather than while descending. On the other hand, in heavy surf (e.g., boulder fields, tangles of downfall, cliffs), fear plays a larger role when facing downhill.

Realize, too, that different riders have different strengths and weaknesses. Some folks can scramble over logs and boulders without a grunt, but they crash head over heels on every switchback turn. Some fly off the steepest drops and others freeze. Some riders climb like the wind and others just blow . . . and walk.

The key to overcoming "technical difficulties" is practice; keep trying. Follow a rider who makes it look easy, and don't hesitate to ask for constructive criticism. Try shifting your weight (good riders move a lot, front to back, side to side, and up and down) and experimenting with balance and momentum. Find a smooth patch of lawn and practice riding as slowly as possible, even balancing at a standstill in a "track stand" (described in the Glossary). This will give you more confidence—and more time to recover or bail out—the next time the trail rears up and bites.

The elevation profiles in this book include difficulty ratings for sections of trails. These ratings don't necessarily describe every foot of the ride but are intended to give a general idea of the technical difficulty of the section. For most trails there is a range of terrain that may be harder or easier than the assigned rating. As with the elevations, not every difficult or easy section can be included on the chart.

A Short Index of Rides

33. Mount Falcon Park Loop
38. Buck Gulch Trail Loop
46. Bergen Peak Loop

Great Downhills—The Need for Speed

4. Hall Ranch Loop
6. Heil Valley Ranch Open Space Loop
7. Walker Ranch Loop
17. Switzerland Trail/Pennsylvania Gulch Loop
20. Jamestown Loop
28. White Ranch Loop
29. Green Mountain Park Loop
32. Apex Park Loop
33. Mount Falcon Park Loop
34. Reynolds Park Loop
36. Deer Creek Canyon Park
38. Buck Gulch Trail Loop
39. Jeremy's Loop
46. Bergen Peak Loop
48. Kenosha Pass South
49. Kenosha Pass North

Barr Lake
State Park Loop

Location: Brighton.

Distance: 9.2-mile loop.

Time: 1 to 2 hours.

Tread: 9.2 miles on doubletrack.

Aerobic level: Easy, the trail is flat as a pancake.

Technical difficulty: 2.

Hazards: Horseback riders, hikers, birdwatchers, and other trail users. Bring extra tubes on this ride.

Highlights: A beautiful, easy ride along the shoreline of Barr Lake. Great views to the Indian Peaks and Rocky Mountain National Park. In fact, you can see for 100 miles in a north and south direction up and down the Front Range. This ride offers a different experience than most rides along the Front Range and offers a welcome relief from the steep hills along the foothills and the mountains. This is one of the best spots along the Front Range for wildlife viewing, and there are several spots along the trail where you can stop and look for the many species of birds and mammals that call this special place home. This is great ride for the whole family to get out and enjoy some excellent riding in a wonderful wildlife area.

Land status: Colorado State Park.

Map: Barr Lake State Park map.

Barr Lake State Park Loop

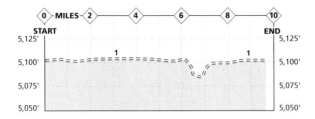

Access: From Denver travel north on I–76 to Bromley Lane (exit 22). Go right on Bromley for 1 mile to Picadilly Road, go right on Picadilly Road for 1.7 miles to the park entrance. The ride starts at the Nature Center.

The Ride

0.0 From the Nature Center and picnic area, travel over the Denver and Hudson Canal via a footbridge.

0.1 Go left on the doubletrack road, with the canal on your left and the lake on the right. The Niedrach Nature Trail veers off to the right. Continue straight.

0.4 Great views to the lake and the mountains. A number of trails on the right access several observation blinds to view wildlife.

1.5 Gazebo Trail shoots to the right. Continue straight.

2.3 Go right on the soft, loose gravel. Great views.

2.6 Go right.

2.9 Eagle nest on the right. Take a break and check out the nest.

4.9 Go right at a gate along the railroad tracks.

5.6 Back on the main trail.

5.9 Arrive at the dam and Bruderlin Stone House. Follow the trail on the north side of the dam, with several hunting blinds on your left.

6.9	Go right.
7.2	Go right.
7.9	Pass through a gate with the boat access and a picnic area on the right.
9.2	Arrive back at the Nature Center.

Devils Backbone Open Space Loop

Location: Loveland.

Distance: 6.5-mile loop.

Time: 1 to 2 hours.

Tread: 6.3 miles on singletrack and 0.2 mile on doubletrack.

Aerobic level: Moderate, with a good stiff climb to gain the upper loop.

Technical difficulty: The ride is mostly in the 2 or 3 range with a couple of technical, rocky sections rated 4.

Hazards: Horseback riders, hikers, birdwatchers, nature lovers, and other trail users. This is a popular trail that sees a fair amount of use from a variety of trail users. Please use caution on the downhills and show common courtesy to other users.

Devils Backbone Open Space Loop

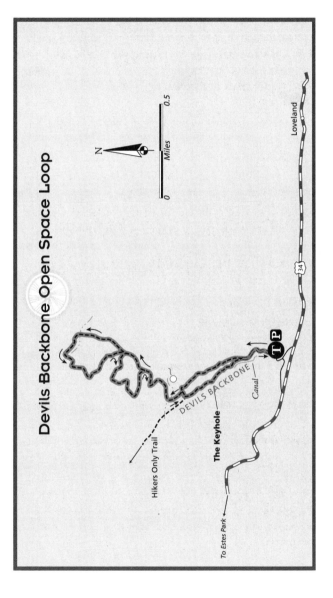

N

Miles
0   0.5

Loveland

34

To Estes Park

Hikers Only Trail

DEVILS BACKBONE

The Keyhole

Canal

T P

Highlights: This is a great ride near the Devils Backbone hogback just west of Loveland. Excellent singletrack riding through hills filled with mahogany oak, cacti, and yuccas. The upper loop has great views to the east and west to Rocky Mountain National Park and the Continental Divide.

Land status: Larimer County Parks and Open Space.

Maps: Larimer County Parks and Open Space/Devils Backbone.

Access: From the junction of U.S. Highway 287 and U.S. Highway 34 in Loveland, go west on U.S. Highway 34 for 4.8 miles to Glade Road. Turn right on Glade Road and make an immediate right turn on Wild Lane. Travel 0.3 mile on Wild Lane to the Devils Backbone trailhead and parking.

The Ride

0.0 From the parking area pedal past the kiosk and follow the signs for Devils Backbone Trail. Go right at

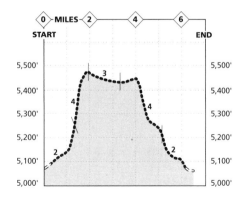

the top of a short hill, through a gate, and then drop down on singletrack to a bridge.

0.3 Reach the bridge and go left on the bike trail. Pedal up to a gate.

0.5 Pedal past the gate and up a short, rocky hill. Enjoy beautiful singletrack riding with views to Devils Backbone to the west.

1.4 Arrive at a trail junction at a fence line and large boulder. Go right and down into a small gulch.

1.6 Cross over a seasonal drainage and begin a steep climb on narrow singletrack. Pedal or walk past a very technical section and crank up to a trail junction.

2.0 Go right and climb up a short hill, then follow the trail into an open meadow filled with tall grasses, mahogany oak, and yuccas.

2.4 Go right through the open meadow on fun singletrack.

2.7 Go right.

3.2 Drop down into a narrow gulch on rocky tread (4). Crank up a steep hill past a flagstone bench. The trail hugs the ridge with steep drop-offs to the right.

3.9 Go right.

4.2 Go right on narrow singletrack along the base of a steep hill.

4.5 Back at a familiar trail junction. Go right and pedal back to the trailhead.

6.5 Back at the parking area.

Lion Gulch

Location: Estes Park.

Distance: 5.8 miles out and back.

Time: 1 to 2.5 hours.

Tread: 5.0 miles on singletrack and 0.8 mile on double-track.

Aerobic level: Strenuous, with several good climbs on technical tread.

Technical difficulty: 4 to 5, depending how long you can stay on the bike.

Hazards: Lion Gulch is a popular trail with hikers and horseback riders. Stay in control and show courtesy to other trail users. A fall on the extremely rocky and technical sections could ruin your day. Be careful!

Highlights: Lion Gulch is for the expert rider looking for a technical challenge. Steep, rocky sections on both the up and down make this a ride that only the hard-core would enjoy. Once reaching Homestead Meadow feel free to explore the many trails leading to various old homesteads.

Land status: Roosevelt National Forest.

Map: Trails Illustrated—Rocky Mountain National Park Number 200.

Access: From Boulder follow U.S. Highway 36 to Lyons. Travel through Lyons and go 12.2 miles on U.S. Highway 36 toward Estes Park to the Lion Gulch trailhead on the left.

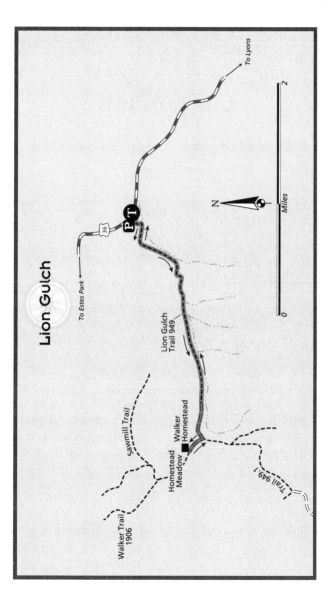

Lion Gulch

To Lyons

To Estes Park

36

P T

Lion Gulch Trail 949

Sawmill Trail

Walker Trail 1906

Homestead Meadow

Walker Homestead

Trail 949.1

N

Miles

0   2

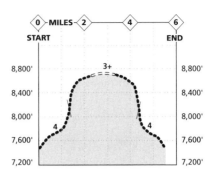

The Ride

0.0 From the parking area drop down past the bathrooms on rocky tread across a small footbridge to a small meadow.

0.2 Go right through the meadow on tight singletrack up to a second footbridge.

0.5 Second footbridge. Cross the footbridge and go left up the steep steps and rocks. Solid 5+ riding up to level terrain. Past the steep section, the trail climbs and descends on some sweet, technical singletrack (4) with U.S. Highway 36 on the right, then makes a quick drop to a small stream.

1.0 Cross the small stream and follow tight tread up and into a small meadow crossing a third footbridge. Make several stream crossings via log bridges (3+) climbing up to the start of a steep hill.

1.7 Reach the start of a steep hill. The creek is now on the right as you climb up on narrow, rocky (4) tread to a stream crossing and small waterfall. The trail pulls steeply away from the creek and gains altitude quickly.

2.0 The last stream crossing and waterfall. Continue climbing on rocky tread with several rock formations on the right and downed trees on the left.

2.3 The trail becomes doubletrack and smooth. Continue straight up through an open meadow to a trail marker.

2.7 Trail junction. Continue straight up to the Walker Homestead.

2.8 Reach the Walker Homestead. Various marked trails shoot out in all direction. Feel free to explore Homestead Meadow and the various homesteads. This ride turns around and returns back to the trailhead from this point.

5.6 Back at the trailhead.

Hall Ranch Loop

Location: Lyons.

Distance: 10.0-mile loop.

Time: 1.5 to 2.5 hours.

Tread: 10.0 miles on singletrack.

Aerobic level: Moderate; a fairly steep climb from the 1-mile to 2-mile mark.

Technical difficulty: 3+.

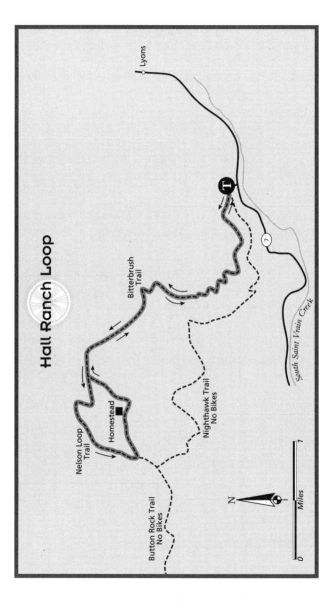

Hall Ranch Loop

Lyons

South Saint Vrain Creek

7

Bitterbrush Trail

Nelson Loop Trail

Homestead

Nighthawk Trail
No Bikes

Button Rock Trail
No Bikes

N

0   1
Miles

Hazards: Horseback riders, hikers, birdwatchers, nature lovers, and other trail users. This is a popular trail and it sees a fair amount of traffic from a variety of trail users. Please use caution on the downhills and show common courtesy with other users.

Highlights: One of the best singletrack rides in the Boulder area. With that said, you will see a crowd on almost any weekend. There is a stiff climb in between mile one and two that has several technical sections on extremely rocky tread. The upper loop around the old Nelson Homestead is absolutely beautiful. Do this ride, preferably on a weekday.

Land status: Boulder County Open Space.

Map: Boulder County Open Space/Hall Ranch.

Access: From Boulder travel west on U.S. Highway 36 to Lyons and a junction with Colorado Highway 7. Go left on Colorado Highway 7 for 1.3 miles to the Hall Ranch Open Space trailhead and parking on the right.

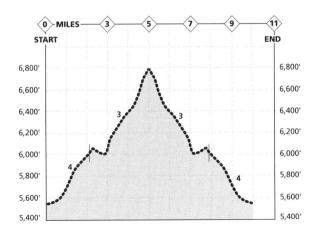

The Ride

0.0 Access Bitterbrush Trail just past the bathrooms near the upper parking area. The trail travels on a wide singletrack through an open meadow on the left and thick stands of mahogany oak on the right. Nice warm-up for the big hill climb ahead.

0.8 Reach an old service road. Continue straight, then drop down into a narrow, rocky section. Begin the climb.

1.2 Rocky tread (3) on tight singletrack.

1.5 More rocky riding.

1.8 Begin a series of tight switchbacks (4) through several rocky sections. The crux of the ride.

2.1 Reach level terrain at a fence line and bench. Beautiful views to the south, west, and east. The trail drops down on fast, fun singletrack that hugs the north edge of the meadow. Nice riding through a stand of young ponderosas leads to a trail junction and the start of the Nelson Loop.

3.8 Go left on the Nelson Loop and climb up through an open meadow to a bridge.

4.0 Cross the footbridge and climb up on tight singletrack to a beautiful open meadow with spectacular views of Mount Meeker and Longs Peak to the west. Pass the old homestead and begin a winding tight descent back to Bitterbrush Trail.

6.2 Reach Bitterbrush Trail and the end of the Nelson Loop. For added mileage turn around and do the loop again, this time in the opposite direction. Complete the ride by following the fast Bitterbrush Trail back to the parking area and trailhead.

10.0 Arrive back at the trailhead.

Rabbit Mountain Loop

Location: 15 miles north of Boulder.

Distance: 5.2-mile loop.

Time: 1 to 1.5 hours.

Tread: 1.2 miles on gravel roads and 4.0 miles on wide singletrack.

Aerobic level: Easy, with a few moderate climbs.

Technical difficulty: 1 on gravel roads; 1 to 3 on singletrack.

Hazards: Watch for other trail users, cacti, and the occasional rattlesnake.

Highlights: Great views of the Continental Divide, Longs Peak, the Flatirons, and the eastern plains.

Land status: Boulder County Open Space.

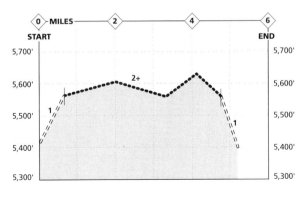

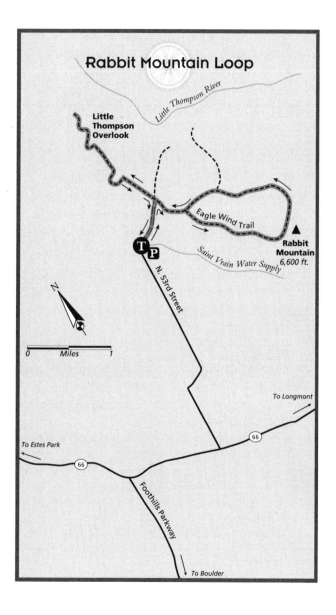

Rabbit Mountain Loop

Little Thompson River

Little Thompson Overlook

Eagle Wind Trail

▲ **Rabbit Mountain 6,600 ft.**

Saint Vrain Water Supply

T P

N. 53rd Street

N

0   Miles   1

To Longmont

To Estes Park

66

66

Foothills Parkway

To Boulder

Map: Zia Design/Boulder County Mountain Bike map.

Access: From Boulder drive about 17 miles north on U.S. Highway 36 to Lyons. Turn right on Colorado Highway 66 and go 1 mile east to 53rd Street. Turn left on 53rd Street and go 2.9 miles north to the trailhead parking lot on the right.

The Ride

0.0 From the parking lot pedal east on the obvious trail leading to a gravel road.

0.1 Go left on the gravel road and begin a moderate climb.

0.6 Go right on Eagle Wind Trail, meandering through a hillside of mahogany shrub.

1.0 Spur trail goes left; continue right. The tread becomes rockier as it cuts through a stand of ponderosa pines.

1.8 Fence line; continue straight.

2.3 Another fence; continue straight.

2.4 Go right and downhill on wide, rocky doubletrack road.

2.9 Trail junction. Go left and spiral downhill to start of Eagle Wind Trail.

3.5 Cross a road and pedal up the rocky Little Thompson Overlook Trail (rated a 3).

4.0 The trail ends at a DO NOT ENTER sign. Turn around and descend the rocky trail to the road.

4.5 Go right, flying down the gravel road toward the trailhead.

5.2 Cruise into the parking lot on 53rd Street.

Heil Valley Ranch Open Space Loop

Location: Boulder.

Distance: 8.1-mile loop.

Time: 1 to 2.5 hours.

Tread: 7.1 miles on singletrack and 1.0 mile on double-track.

Aerobic level: Moderate; there is a fair amount of climbing getting to the overlook.

Technical difficulty: 3.

Hazards: Horseback riders, hikers, birdwatchers, nature lovers, and other trail users. This is a popular trail and it sees a fair amount of use from a variety of trail users. Please use caution on the downhills and show common courtesy to other users.

Highlights: A new trail in new open space just 8 miles from Boulder. Excellent singletrack riding through beautiful ponderosas with great views in all directions. This is a fantastic ride through the foothills just north of Boulder that offers good singletrack riding with a stiff climb to start the ride. The views from the overlook are just stunning.

Land status: Boulder County Open Space.

Maps: Boulder County Open Space/Heil Valley Open Space.

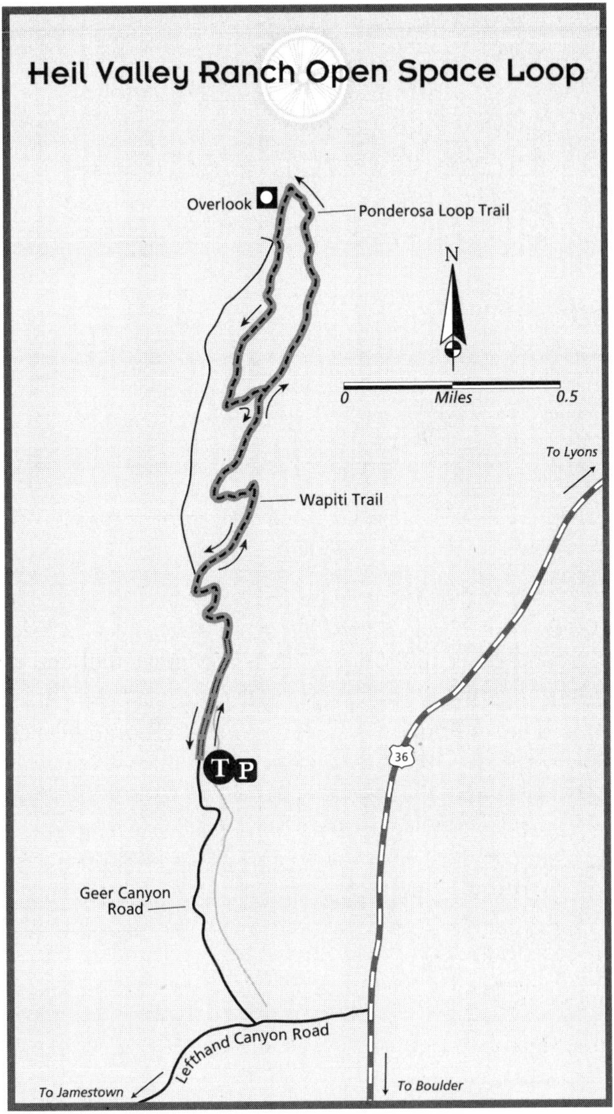

Heil Valley Ranch Open Space Loop

Overlook

Ponderosa Loop Trail

N

0   Miles   0.5

Wapiti Trail

To Lyons

36

T P

Geer Canyon
Road

Lefthand Canyon Road

To Jamestown

To Boulder

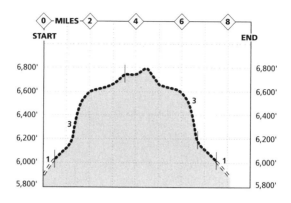

Access: From Boulder travel west on U.S. Highway 36 to Lefthand Canyon Road. Go left on Lefthand Canyon Road and travel 0.5 mile to Geer Canyon Road on the right. Follow Geer Canyon Road for 1.3 miles to the trailhead and parking area. The ride starts here.

The Ride

0.0 From the parking area pedal past the kiosk up a short hill following the signs for Wapiti Trail. Follow the service road up to a junction with Wapiti Trail.

0.5 Go left on Wapiti Trail through an open meadow filled with prairie dog houses. The trail winds to the right and climbs up to a footbridge.

0.7 Cross the footbridge, climb past an open meadow with views to the south, and head into the ponderosas. Excellent singletrack riding leads to a service road.

1.4 Cross the road and pedal up a short, rocky hill to an old homestead ruin.

1.8 At the ruin the trail goes left and climbs up to Ponderosa Loop Trail.

2.7 Reach Ponderosa Loop Trail. Go right and up for a short distance. The trail drops down through an open meadow and heads in a northerly direction. The trail heads to the west and back into the ponderosas. Enjoy great riding and a slight hill climb up to a service road.

3.5 Cross the service road and pedal to the overlook.

3.9 Reach the overlook and take a break. Take in the spectacular views to Lyons and the north. Sit on the bench and chill out. After your break, continue on Ponderosa Loop Trail, now heading in a westerly direction. Good views to Mount Meeker and Longs Peak add to the experience. The trail winds back to the east and makes a great downhill run back to Wapiti Trail.

5.4 Back at Wapiti Trail and the end of Ponderosa Loop Trail. For extra mileage do the Ponderosa Loop Trail again in the opposite direction. Go right on Wapiti Trail and fly back to the trailhead. Keep your speed in check and show courtesy to other trail users.

8.1 Back at the trailhead.

Walker Ranch Loop

Location: 8 miles west of Boulder, off Flagstaff Road.

Distance: 7.4-mile loop.

Time: 1.5 to 3.5 hours.

Tread: 3.5 miles on doubletrack and 3.9 miles on single-track.

Aerobic level: Strenuous, with several short, low-gear climbs.

Technical difficulty: 3 to 4 on doubletrack; 4 to 4+ on singletrack.

Hazards: Some sections of the trail are extremely rocky, with bad landings. Dismount and walk your bike down the steep steps to South Boulder Creek. Watch out for other bikers and trail users. This ride is popular and weekends can be crowded.

Highlights: Great riding with easy access from Boulder. Beautiful views of Eldorado State Park and the Indian Peaks. See Ride 8 for more riding in the area.

Land status: Boulder County Open Space.

Map: Boulder County Open Space.

Access: From the intersection of Broadway and Baseline Road in Boulder, go 7.5 miles west on Baseline Road, beyond Flagstaff Mountain. Baseline Road becomes Flagstaff Road just beyond 6th Street. Look for Walker

Walker Ranch Loop, Meyers Homestead Trail, Flagstaff Road, Marshall Mesa/Community Ditch Trail

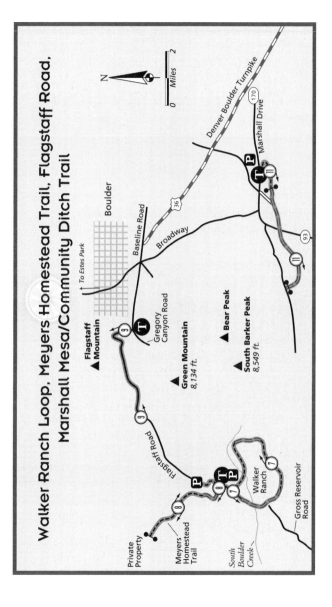

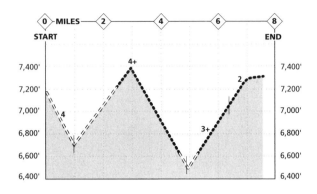

Ranch signs and turn left into the parking area for the South Boulder Creek trailhead.

The Ride

0.0 Cruise down South Boulder Trail—a great downhill with some ruts and rocky sections.

1.0 Cross South Boulder Creek and enjoy an all-too-brief run along this beautiful stream.

1.5 Cross over a bridge and turn left, up a short but steep hill. Then continue the strenuous climb over some short, rocky sections (4+) to the top of a small ridge. Breeze down a short hill only to rebound up another short, steep section. Continue past a gate to Gross Reservoir Road.

2.4 Turn left on Gross Reservoir Road, and pedal 0.1 mile, looking on the left for a trail.

2.5 Turn left on the singletrack, go up a short hill, and bear left onto awesome, winding singletrack with some level 5 rock gardens.

4.5 Caution! If you value your life, dismount and carry your bike down the steep, rocky steps to South Boulder Creek.

4.7 Cross the bridge and go left, up strenuous, loose, sandy, and steep doubletrack (4-).

5.8 Turn left on Columbine Gulch Trail. Follow this steep, tight singletrack (it's no sin to walk this stretch), pedaling through dense pine forest to an obvious ridge. The trail veers right.

6.8 Go right on singletrack, over more rocky tread (4), and down a short hill toward the trailhead.

7.4 Cross over the gate to the parking lot and your car.

Meyers Homestead Trail

Location: 8 miles west of Boulder. See map on page 41.

Distance: 5.2 miles out and back.

Time: 45 minutes to 1.5 hours.

Tread: 2.0 miles on dirt road, 1.5 miles on doubletrack, and 1.7 miles on singletrack.

Aerobic level: Mostly moderate, with one short climb.

Technical difficulty: 1 to 2 on dirt road; 1 to 3 on double- and singletrack.

Hazards: Watch for other trail users; ride in control, especially on the downhill on the return trip to the trailhead.

Highlights: Good beginner's trail with nice views of Indian Peaks. Readily accessible from Boulder.

Land status: Boulder County Open Space.

Map: Boulder County Open Space/Walker Ranch.

Access: From the intersection of Broadway and Baseline Road in Boulder, drive 7.5 miles west on Baseline Road and turn right into the Meyers Gulch trailhead parking lot.

The Ride

0.0 From the parking lot pedal through the gate and roll downhill on a wide dirt road.

0.6 Pass an old barn on the left, then climb gradually as the trail switches from doubletrack to singletrack. Come to an intersection with an old service road on the right. Go straight.

1.3 Continue climbing. The trail grows rockier near the top.

2.6 Roll up to a fenced and posted private property boundary. Turn around and cruise downhill back to the trailhead.

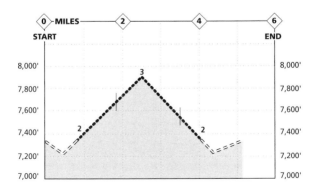

5.2 Roll into the parking lot at the Meyers Gulch trail-head.

Flagstaff Road

Location: 2 miles southwest of downtown Boulder. See map on page 41.

Distance: 9.0 miles out and back.

Time: 1 to 2 hours.

Tread: 9.0 miles on paved road.

Aerobic level: Moderate, with a few steep sections.

Technical difficulty: None.

Hazards: Watch for traffic and a wide assortment of runners, bikers, and other Boulder body-buffers who train on this popular road.

Highlights: Close to Boulder, a good hill climb with great views of the Flatirons and Boulder. Access to Rides 7 and 8.

Land status: Boulder County.

Map: Zia Design/Boulder County Mountain Bike map.

Access: From the intersection of Broadway and Baseline Road in Boulder, pedal or drive 1.4 miles west on Baseline Road to the Gregory Canyon trailhead. Odometer readings begin at the intersection of Baseline Road and Gregory Canyon Road.

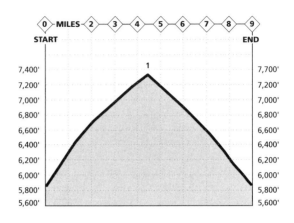

The Ride

0.0 Head west up Flagstaff Road, climbing a steep grade to a fee station on the right (no charge for cyclists).

0.5 Continue up the road, enjoying great views of the Flatirons as the road bends right.

1.1 Pedal past a parking area on the right.

1.7 Continue climbing, and try to keep one eye on the road while the other one wanders to more great panoramic views.

2.3 The grade eases.

2.8 Flagstaff Amphitheater on the right.

3.5 Crank up a set of steep switchbacks to Flagstaff Overlook and spectacular views of the Indian Peaks.

3.8 Continue uphill, looping through more steep switchbacks.

4.3 Grind through the last switchbacks to the top.

4.5 Welcome to the summit! Catch your breath and retrace your route back to Gregory Canyon Road.

9.0 What a great downhill! No wonder some people still own road bikes. Crank right into Gregory Canyon if you left a vehicle there, or buzz back down Baseline into town.

Foothills Trail/Boulder Valley Ranch Trail

Location: 2 miles north of downtown Boulder.

Distance: 13.2 miles out and back.

Time: 1 to 2 hours.

Tread: 4.0 miles on singletrack, 2.2 miles on paved roads, and 7.0 miles on dirt roads.

Aerobic level: Moderate.

Technical difficulty: 3 on singletrack; 2 on dirt roads; 1 on paved roads.

Hazards: Watch for other trail users, including horses. Look both ways for traffic when crossing paved roads.

Highlights: An excellent workout close to Boulder. Great beginner's ride with wonderful views of surrounding mountains and plains.

Land status: Boulder County Open Space.

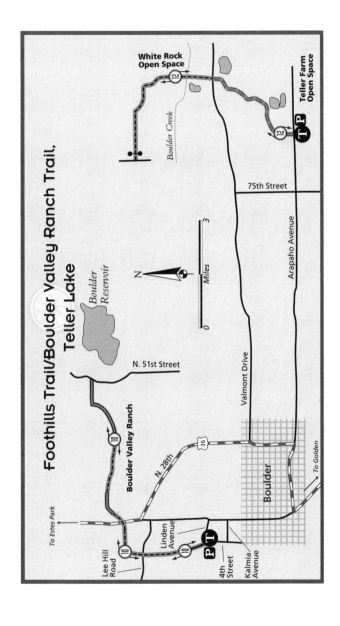

Foothills Trail/Boulder Valley Ranch Trail, Teller Lake

White Rock Open Space

Teller Farm Open Space

Boulder Creek

75th Street

Arapaho Avenue

Boulder Reservoir

N

Miles

0   3

N. 51st Street

Valmont Drive

Boulder Valley Ranch

N. 28th

36

Boulder

To Golden

To Estes Park

Lee Hill Road

Linden Avenue

4th Street

Kalmia Avenue

Map: Zia Design/Boulder County Bike map.

Access: From the intersection of Broadway and Kalmia Avenue in Boulder, turn left on Kalmia and pedal 0.5 mile west to 4th Street. Turn right onto 4th Street and go about 0.25 mile to the paved bike path. Odometer readings start here.

The Ride

0.0 Pedal north on the paved bike path to Linden Avenue. (CAUTION: Watch for traffic.) Cross Linden and go left up Wonderland Drive.

0.2 Pedal left up the paved path.

0.3 Go left at a three-way intersection.

0.5 Pedal across a paved road.

0.6 The trail splits; go left around Wonderland Lake.

0.9 Another split in the trail. Go left, up a short hill, and cruise on singletrack to a parking area.

1.8 Cross Lee Hill Road (CAUTION!) to the trail on the other side, and go left to a short hill.

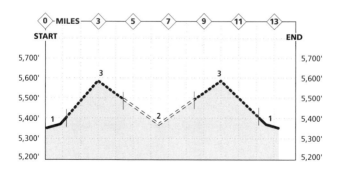

2.2	Crank up a short, rocky section (3) that tops out on a low ridge. Then spin down a short hill with steps (3) to a gate.
2.5	Go right on awesome singletrack that crosses under U.S. Highway 36 to another trailhead parking area.
3.0	Go left up a dirt road.
3.1	The road forks; go right.
3.2	Go right again at another fork.
3.5	Pedal past an iron gate and onto Eagle Trail.
4.2	Pass through a gate (please close it behind you) and go left on singletrack.
4.4	Junction with Mesa Trail on the right. Go left on great singletrack. Drop down a short hill to a wide dirt path. The path skirts a pond and then grunts to the top of a short hill.
5.9	Go right on a wide dirt road to Boulder Reservoir (swimming, boating, and fishing).
6.6	Turn around and retrace your route to the Linden Avenue trailhead.
13.2	Cross Linden to 4th Street and pedal home from here.

Marshall Mesa/ Community Ditch Trail

Location: 2 miles south of Boulder. See map on page 41.

Distance: 8.8 miles out and back.

Time: 1 to 2 hours.

Tread: 1.6 miles on singletrack and 7.2 miles on wide doubletrack.

Aerobic level: Easy, with a few moderate climbs.

Technical difficulty: 1 to 3+ on singletrack; 1 to 2+ on doubletrack.

Hazards: Watch for other trail users. Use extra caution crossing Colorado Highway 93 at mile 2.1. Please close all gates behind you.

Highlights: Excellent beginner's ride close to Boulder. Great views of the Flatirons and Indian Peaks. Can be biked most of the year. Also see Ride 9, Flagstaff Road.

Land status: Boulder County Open Space.

Map: Zia Design/Boulder County Mountain Bike map.

Access: From the intersection of Broadway and Table Mesa Road in Boulder, pedal or drive south on Broadway to Colorado Highway 170 (Marshall Drive). Turn left on Colorado Highway 170 to the Marshall Mesa trailhead parking lot on the right.

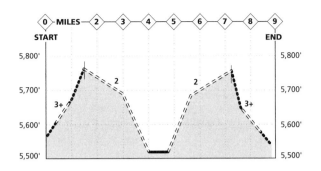

The Ride

0.0 From the parking lot pedal past a gate and up a wide dirt trail going south.

0.1 Cross a small footbridge and roll onto sweet single-track that winds up and around to the top of a small hill.

0.5 Go right to stay on the wide dirt trail.

0.7 A three-way trail junction. Turn right and cruise along the Community Ditch.

1.4 Continue straight around a gate and continue along the Community Ditch.

1.6 Pedal over a bridge and up a short, steep section with rock steps and water bars (3+).

1.8 Go right and downhill on a gravel road.

2.1 Skirt another gate and cross Colorado Highway 93. (CAUTION: Look both ways for traffic.) The trail continues from the other side of the road, following the Community Ditch to another gate.

2.3 Pedal along the ditch through a broad, open field with spectacular views of the Flatirons.

3.6 Continue straight around another gate.

3.9 Junction with Doudy Draw Trail on the left. Go right and slightly downhill to a picnic area.

4.1 Continue straight, past the picnic area. The trail is paved here and rolls downhill to the Doudy Draw trailhead parking lot on Eldorado Springs Drive.

4.4 Cruise into the parking lot and take a short break before retracing your route back to the Marshall Mesa trailhead.

8.8 Welcome back to the Marshall Mesa trailhead parking lot and your car.

Teller Lake

Location: 8 miles east of Boulder. See map on page 48.

Distance: 12.2 miles out and back.

Time: 1 to 1.5 hours.

Tread: 10.0 miles on hardpacked farm roads and 2.2 miles on singletrack.

Aerobic level: Easy, with a few moderate climbs.

Technical difficulty: 1 to 2+ on dirt roads; 1 to 2+ on singletrack.

Hazards: Watch for other trail users; please close all gates.

Highlights: Great beginner's ride. Excellent wildlife viewing and beautiful views of the Flatirons and Indian Peaks. Beautiful riding on old farm roads and some cow paths. This is a great ride that can be ridden year round.

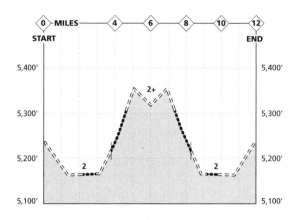

Land status: Boulder County Open Space.

Map: Zia Design/Boulder County Mountain Bike map.

Access: From the intersection of Broadway and Arapaho Avenue in Boulder, pedal or drive 7 miles east on Arapaho to 75th Street. Continue straight 0.5 mile on Arapaho to the Teller Lake trailhead entrance. Turn left and go 1 mile to the trailhead parking lot.

The Ride

0.0 From the parking lot go past a gate onto wide gravel doubletrack.

0.2 Junction with a trail on the left. Go straight on the gravel doubletrack as it winds along an irrigation ditch to a gate.

0.6 Pedal straight on a dirt road, passing houses on the right.

1.0 Pedal through a gate and along another irrigation ditch.

1.6 Cross a bridge and go gently downhill on the wide dirt road, passing an oil derrick.

2.1 Pedal past another gate to a parking area on the right. Pick up the well-marked trail on the north end of the parking area.

2.3 The trail drops onto Valmont Road. (CAUTION: Watch for traffic.) The well-marked trail continues on the other side. Follow the trail, winding around some private farms.

2.7 Railroad crossing. Pedal over the tracks and follow the dirt road past beautiful ponds on the left.

3.1 Cross a bridge and pedal to a singletrack trail on the right.

3.3 Follow the singletrack up a short hill, where the trail widens to doubletrack.

3.5 Follow the obvious trail, where the trail becomes singletrack again.

4.0 Go down fun singletrack, then up a short hill.

4.3 Cross a paved road (actually a private driveway) and continue on singletrack.

4.4 Three-way trail junction. Go left on Gunbarrel Trail, pedaling uphill through a beautiful field.

4.9 Go right, winding around open fields to a large water tank.

5.4 Continue straight past the water tank, down a fast dirt road to the end of the trail.

6.1 Turn your bike around and retrace your tire tracks back to the Teller Lake trailhead.

12.2 Crank your way past the gate to the Teller Lake trailhead.

Logan Mill Road

Location: 4 miles west of Boulder.

Distance: 13.8 miles out and back.

Time: 1.5 to 2.5 hours.

Tread: 7.6 miles on paved roads and 6.2 miles on dirt roads.

Aerobic level: Moderate, with a long climb up Logan Mill Road.

Technical difficulty: 1 on paved roads; 1 to 2+ on dirt roads.

Hazards: Watch for traffic on Fourmile Canyon Road. The climb up Logan Mill Road crosses private property; please stay on the road.

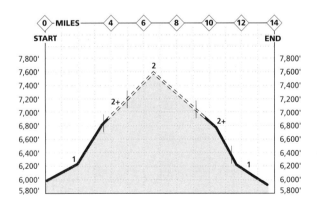

Logan Mill Road, Betasso Reserve Loop

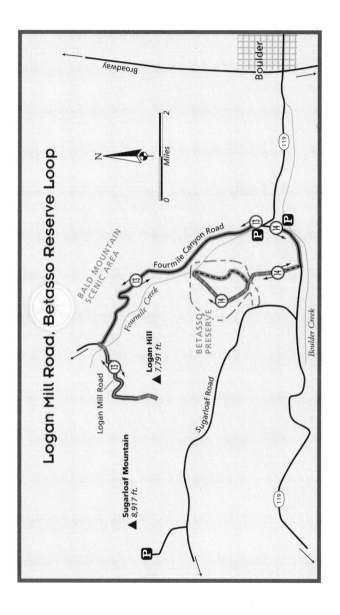

Highlights: A great hill climb; close to Boulder; excellent views; and good downhill on a hard-packed dirt road. Also see Ride 14.

Land status: Boulder County.

Map: Zia Design/Boulder County Mountain Bike map.

Access: From Broadway and Canyon Road (Colorado Highway 119) in Boulder, drive or pedal 2.9 miles west on Canyon Road to a large pullout parking area on the left.

The Ride

0.0 Cross Colorado Highway 119 (CAUTION: Watch for traffic!) to Fourmile Canyon Road. Odometer reading starts here. Pedal up paved Fourmile Canyon Road.

1.9 Poorman's Road goes left. Continue on Fourmile Canyon Road.

3.2 Arroyo Chico Road goes right. Continue up Fourmile Canyon Road.

3.8 Turn left on Logan Mill Road and begin an extended climb on a well-maintained dirt grade.

4.7 The road splits. Go right on rockier tread.

5.0 Spur road on the right. Stay straight on the main road.

6.2 The road bends near two houses. Continue straight past the houses, up a steep but short hill, to a junction with Arkansas Mountain Road on the right.

6.7 Go right, up a short hill, to a flat area with great views of Sugarloaf Mountain.

6.9 Stop here, enjoy the views, then turn your bike around and retrace your route back to Colorado Highway 119.

13.8 Colorado Highway 119 and the parking area.

Betasso Preserve Loop

Location: 4 miles west of Boulder. See map on page 57.

Distance: 7.4-mile loop.

Time: 1 to 2 hours.

Tread: 2.4 miles on paved road, 2.4 miles on doubletrack, and 2.6 miles on singletrack.

Aerobic level: Moderate, with a long climb up to Betasso Preserve.

Technical difficulty: 1 on paved roads; 2 to 4+ on singletrack; 2 to 4+ on doubletrack.

Hazards: The downhill back to Canyon Road (Colorado Highway 119) is very steep and loose. Watch for traffic on Canyon Road. *Mountain bikes are not allowed in Betasso Preserve on Wednesday and Saturday throughout the year. Please abide by this rule. Don't spoil it for other cyclists.*

Highlights: Excellent singletrack around Betasso Preserve. This ride is a good, quick workout close to Boulder. Hammerheads can do laps around Betasso to increase mileage. Also see Ride 13.

Land status: Boulder County Open Space.

Map: Zia Design/Boulder County Mountain Bike map.

Access: From Broadway and Canyon Road (Colorado Highway 119) in Boulder, drive or pedal 2.9 miles west on Canyon Road to a large pullout parking area on the left. The mileage readings start here.

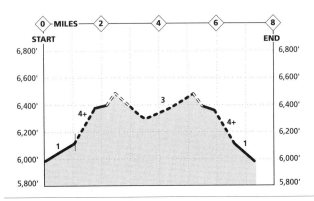

The Ride

0.0 From the parking pullout pedal up Canyon Road, bearing left to stay on Colorado Highway 119 where Fourmile Canyon Road splits right.

1.0 Just before a tunnel, pedal onto singletrack going right and uphill. The tread is steep, rocky, and loose—a 4+.

1.4 Bear right and crank through several sections of steep and technical (4) riding up to an old road and iron gate.

1.9 The trail ends at an iron gate. Look for traffic, then pedal left onto a paved road.

2.0 Turn right onto a gravel road heading into Betasso Preserve to the west end parking area on the left.

2.1 Take the wide trail past the OPEN SPACE sign.

2.2 Go right past a gate, then up a short hill on wide doubletrack.

2.4 Junction with Canyon Loop Trail. Cruise down this fast, wide doubletrack.

2.9 Climb a short hill, then go right on tight single-track. Hang on for a steep downhill.

3.7 Cross a small creek and traverse the hillside.

4.0 Cross another small creek and climb steadily up beautiful singletrack.

4.9 Go straight past an iron gate on a dirt road to the west end parking area.

5.3 From the parking area, either take another lap around Betasso Preserve, or retrace your route to Colorado Highway 119. Be careful on the downhill and keep your speed in check.

6.4 Go left on Colorado Highway 119, down past the Red Lion Inn.

7.4 Back at the pullout on Canyon Road.

Rattlesnake Gulch

Location: 6 miles south of Boulder.

Distance: 7.6 miles out and back.

Time: 1 to 2 hours.

Tread: 2.0 miles on paved road, 2.2 miles on packed dirt road, and 3.4 miles on singletrack.

Aerobic level: Strenuous, with a 1,200-foot elevation gain in 2 miles.

Technical difficulty: 1 on paved road; 1 to 2 on dirt roads; 2 to 3+ on singletrack.

Hazards: Watch for traffic on roads and other trail users on singletrack. This is a popular trail on weekends.

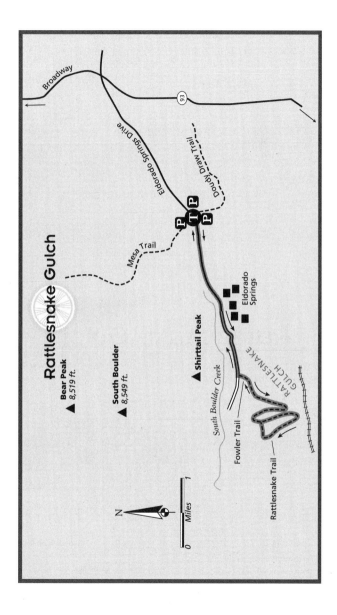

Rattlesnake Gulch

Broadway

93

Eldorado Springs Drive

Doudy Draw Trail

P T P

Mesa Trail

▲ Bear Peak
8,519 ft.

▲ South Boulder
8,549 ft.

▲ Shirttail Peak

Eldorado Springs

South Boulder Creek

Fowler Trail

RATTLESNAKE GULCH

Rattlesnake Trail

N

0   Miles   1

Highlights: Close to Boulder, this ride has a little of every-thing. Diehards will enjoy the steep, tight climbing on the singletrack up Rattlesnake Gulch. Also see Ride 11.

Land status: Public roads; Eldorado State Park.

Map: Zia Design/Boulder County Mountain Bike map.

Access: From the intersection of Broadway and Baseline Road in Boulder, bike or drive 3 miles south on Broadway (Colorado Highway 93). Turn right and go 3 miles on Eldorado Springs Drive (Colorado Highway 170) to the Doudy Draw trailhead on the left. The mileage count starts here.

The Ride

0.0 From the trailhead turn left on Eldorado Springs Drive. (CAUTION: Watch for heavy traffic.) Pedal west on paved road to the town of Eldorado Springs.

1.0 The road turns to dirt as it passes the world-famous Eldorado Springs pool. Cross the bridge over South

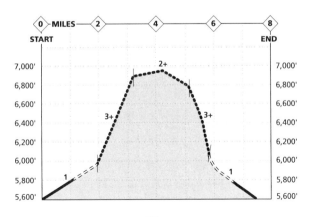

Boulder Creek.

1.4 Pedal up to the entrance to Eldorado State Park. Cyclists pay a $1.00 entrance fee. Begin climbing on the dirt road, past rock walls that lure rock climbers from around the world.

2.0 Go left on Fowler Trail.

2.2 Pedal right onto Rattlesnake Gulch Trail, through a short, rocky section (3+). Then scramble up loose rocky tread to where the trail levels out.

2.4 The trail, now singletrack, winds steeply up Rattlesnake Gulch to an opening with beautiful views north, west, and east.

3.4 The trail splits. Go right on great singletrack to the ruins of an old hotel.

3.7 A spur trail goes right; continue left on singletrack.

4.1 Go right and downhill on tight singletrack to Fowler Trail.

5.6 Go right on the dirt road to return to the Doudy Draw trailhead.

7.6 Turn right to roll up to the trailhead and your car.

Switzerland Trail

Location: Boulder.

Distance: 15.0 miles out and back.

Time: 1 to 2 hours.

Tread: 15.0 miles on rough doubletrack.

Aerobic level: Moderate, with a steady climb up to the Mt. Alto Picnic Grounds.

Technical difficulty: 2–3.

Hazards: Four-wheel-drive vehicle users, hikers, bird-watchers, nature lovers, and other trail users. This is a popular trail and it sees a fair amount of use from a variety of trail users. Please use caution on the downhills and show common courtesy to other users.

Highlights: This is a good ride on somewhat rocky tread just outside Boulder. The first part of the trail drops steeply to the town of Sunset on very rocky tread. The ride then makes a steady climb from Sunset up to the Mt. Alto Picnic Grounds, the turnaround point for this ride description. You can extend your riding time and mileage by following Switzerland Trail past the town of Gold Hill and continuing on Switzerland Trail for over 3 miles, where the trail ends in a talus field.

Land status: Roosevelt National Forest.

Maps: Zia Design/Boulder County Bike map; Trail Illustrated—Indian Peaks #103.

Switzerland Trail

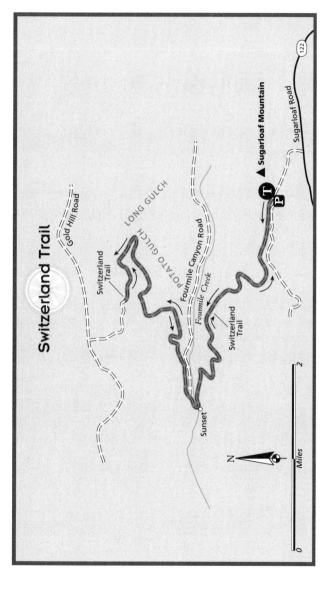

Gold Hill Road

Switzerland Trail

LONG GULCH

POTATO GULCH

Fourmile Canyon Road

Fourmile Creek

Switzerland Trail

Sunset

Sugarloaf Mountain ▲

T
P

Sugarloaf Road

122

N

Miles

0   2

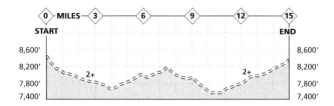

Access: From the intersection of Broadway and Canyon Road (Colorado Highway 119) in Boulder, travel west on Canyon Road for 5.5 miles to Magnolia Road (County Road 122). Turn right on Magnolia Road and travel 4.5 miles to a turnoff on the right for the Switzerland trailhead. Travel 1 mile up to the trailhead and a parking area. The ride starts here.

The Ride

0.0 Switzerland Trail starts at the far end (north) of the parking area. Drop down the doubletrack road and begin an extended downhill section on rocky tread. Pass Bear Gulch Trail on the left and reach the village of Sunset and Forest Road 109.

4.0 Arrive at Sunset. Bear right following Forest Road 109 and begin a steady climb up through Potato Gulch to the Mt. Alto Picnic Grounds.

4.2 Pass Fourmile Canyon Road on the right.

7.5 Reach the Mt. Alto Picnic Grounds and the turnaround point.

15.0 Back to Switzerland Trail parking area.

Switzerland Trail/ Pennsylvania Gulch Loop

Location: 8 miles northwest of Boulder.

Distance: 9.6-mile loop.

Time: 1 to 2 hours.

Tread: 9.6 miles on four-wheel-drive roads.

Aerobic level: Easy, with a long, steady climb from the town of Sunset (at mile 5.7) back to the trailhead.

Technical difficulty: 1 to 4+; the 4+ can be avoided by walking parts of the trail down Pennsylvania Gulch.

Hazards: Watch for four-wheel-drive traffic and other trail users. The trail down Pennsylvania Gulch is steep, rocky, and technical.

Highlights: Great beginner's ride, except for a short section on Pennsylvania Gulch. Excellent views of the Indian Peaks and surrounding mountains. Good workout, close to Boulder. Also see rides 16, 18, and 19.

Land status: Roosevelt National Forest.

Map: Zia design/Boulder County Mountain Bike map.

Access: From the intersection of Broadway and Canyon Road (Colorado Highway 119) in Boulder, go 5.1 miles west on Canyon Road to Sugarloaf Road. Turn right and

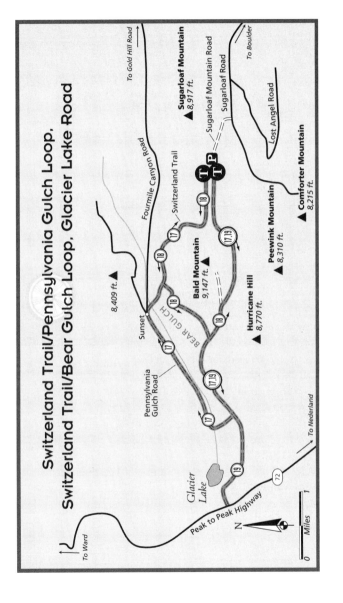

Switzerland Trail/Pennsylvania Gulch Loop,
Switzerland Trail/Bear Gulch Loop, Glacier Lake Road

To Gold Hill Road

Sugarloaf Mountain
▲ 8,917 ft.

To Boulder

Sugarloaf Mountain Road

Sugarloaf Road

Lost Angel Road

Fourmile Canyon Road

Switzerland Trail

T
P
T

18

17

18

17,19

Bald Mountain
▲ 9,147 ft.

Peewink Mountain
▲ 8,310 ft.

Comforter Mountain
▲ 8,215 ft.

18

BEAR GULCH

18

17

Sunset

18

Hurricane Hill
▲ 8,770 ft.

8,409 ft. ▲

17,19

Pennsylvania
Gulch Road

17

19

Glacier
Lake

72

Peak to Peak Highway

To Nederland

To Ward

N

0   Miles   1

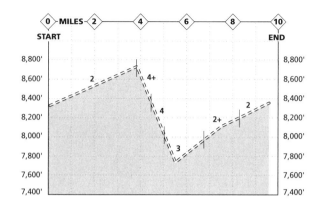

drive 5 miles on Sugarloaf Road to Sugarloaf Mountain Road. Turn right and go 1 mile to the parking lot.

The Ride

0.0 From the parking lot pedal west on the wide, four-wheel-drive road on the left (Forest Road 120), which leads to Glacier Lake.

0.3 Spur road goes left; continue straight.

0.4 Spur road goes left; continue straight.

0.6 Spur road goes left; continue straight.

1.0 Four-way intersection; continue straight.

1.8 Great views of the Indian Peaks and surrounding foothills.

2.3 A road goes right (up to Bald Mountain); continue straight.

2.4 A road goes right (to Bear Gulch); continue straight. The tread becomes rocky as the road winds among aspen and pine.

3.7 Spur road goes left; continue straight.

4.0 Spur road goes left; continue straight.

4.1 Turn right onto Pennsylvania Gulch Road (Forest Road 109) and begin a technical descent along this rough, loose, rocky road.

4.2 Road becomes extremely rocky (4 to 4+) as it drops to a three-way trail junction.

4.5 Go right as the road becomes even more steep and rocky (4+) and descends to an old mine on the right.

5.0 Continue down the road (now 3+), enjoying smoother tread.

5.7 The town of Sunset is on the left. Go right on Switzerland Trail and gear down for a steady climb toward the trailhead.

6.5 Bear Gulch Road goes right; continue straight.

6.8 Spur road goes right; continue straight.

7.5 Tread becomes rockier; continue straight to a junction with a road on the left.

8.3 Go straight as the road gently climbs to the parking area.

9.6 Roll into the trailhead parking lot.

Switzerland Trail/
Bear Gulch Loop

Location: 8 miles northwest of Boulder. See map on page 69.

Distance: 8.8-mile loop.

Time: 1.5 to 2.5 hours.

Tread: 8.8 miles on dirt four-wheel-drive roads.

Aerobic level: Mostly moderate, with a long climb out of Bear Gulch.

Technical difficulty: 1 to 3; short sections of 4 to 5 out of Bear Gulch.

Hazards: Watch for four-wheel-drive traffic and other cyclists.

Highlights: Great views of the Indian Peaks; good workout close to Boulder. Also see rides 16, 17, and 19.

Land status: Roosevelt National Forest.

Maps: Roosevelt National Forest; Trails Illustrated—Gold Hill/Indian Peaks.

Access: From the intersection of Broadway and Canyon Road (Colorado Highway 119) in Boulder, drive 5.1 miles west on Canyon Road to Sugarloaf Road. Turn right and go 5 miles on Sugarloaf Road to Sugarloaf Mountain Road. Turn right and go 1 mile to the parking lot.

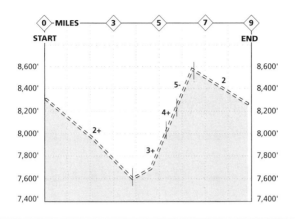

The Ride

0.0 From the parking lot pedal west to Switzerland Trail, a somewhat rocky four-wheel-drive road. Descend gradually to the scenic village of Sunset and the intersection with Pennsylvania Gulch Road (Forest Road 109) on the right.

4.0 Turn around and pedal back up Switzerland Trail to Bear Creek.

4.7 Turn right on Bear Gulch Road and crank up a steep, rocky hill (a solid 4) where the creek crosses the road.

5.1 Climb a short steep section (4).

5.3 The road forks. Go left up the hideously steep and rocky (5) four-wheel-drive road to the top of a small ridge. Most riders push their bikes on this section.

5.7 Roll down a short hill, then resume climbing as the road sweeps into a meadow.

5.9 Go left, crossing a stream to an open area and start an extended climb over roots and babyhead-sized rocks (5).

73

6.6 Go left on the wide Glacier Lake Trail Road (County Road 120) to a three-way intersection. Continue straight on this sporadically rocky road.

8.8 Turn left into the trailhead parking lot.

Glacier Lake Road

Location: 8 miles northwest of Boulder. See map on page 69.

Distance: 11.0 miles out and back.

Time: 1 to 2 hours.

Tread: 11.0 miles on wide dirt roads.

Aerobic level: Easy.

Technical difficulty: 1.

Hazards: Watch for traffic, bikers, and other carbon-based life forms that use this popular road.

Highlights: Great beginner's ride with excellent views of the Indian Peaks. Optional links to other local roads for longer rides. See Rides 16, 17, and 18.

Land status: Roosevelt National Forest.

Map: Trails Illustrated—Gold Hill/Indian Peaks.

Access: From the intersection of Broadway and Canyon Road (Colorado Highway 119) in Boulder, drive 5.1 miles west on Canyon Road to Sugarloaf Road. Turn right and go

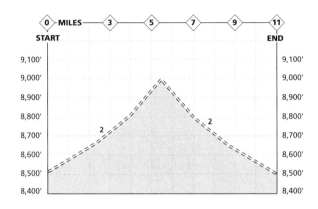

5 miles on Sugarloaf Road to Sugarloaf Mountain Road. Turn right and go 1 mile to the parking lot.

The Ride

0.0 From the parking lot pedal west on the wide, four-wheel-drive road on the left (Forest Road 120), which leads to Glacier Lake.

0.3 Spur road on the left; continue straight.

0.4 Spur road on the left; continue straight.

0.6 Spur road on the left; continue straight.

1.0 Four-way intersection; continue straight.

1.8 Great views of the Indian Peaks and surrounding foothills.

2.3 A road goes right (up to Bald Mountain); continue straight.

2.4 A road goes right (to Bear Gulch); continue straight. The tread becomes rocky as the road winds among aspen and pine.

3.7 Spur road on the left; continue straight.

4.0 Spur road on the left; continue straight.

4.1 Pennsylvania Gulch Road (Forest Road 109) on the right; stay left.

5.5 Junction with Colorado Highway 72. Turn around and retrace your route to the trailhead.

11.0 Back at the trailhead.

Jamestown Loop

Location: 12 miles northwest of Boulder, near the village of Jamestown.

Distance: 9.5-mile loop.

Time: 1.5 to 3 hours.

Tread: 0.5 mile on paved road, 0.5 mile on maintained dirt road, and 8.0 miles on four-wheel-drive roads.

Aerobic level: Mostly moderate, with several strenuous climbs.

Technical difficulty: 1 on paved road; 1 to 5- on four-wheel-drive roads.

Hazards: Watch for four-wheel-drive traffic. The stream crossing at mile 3 can be risky during spring runoff. The downhill back into Jamestown is steep, rocky, and dangerous.

Highlights: Great uphill along James Creek; nice views of the Indian Peaks; and good, rocky, technical downhill for adrenaline junkies. Many trails criss-cross this area. Feel free to explore after doing this loop.

Jamestown Loop, Ceran Saint Vrain Loop, Sourdough Trail/Camp Dick, Buchanan Pass/Camp Dick Loop

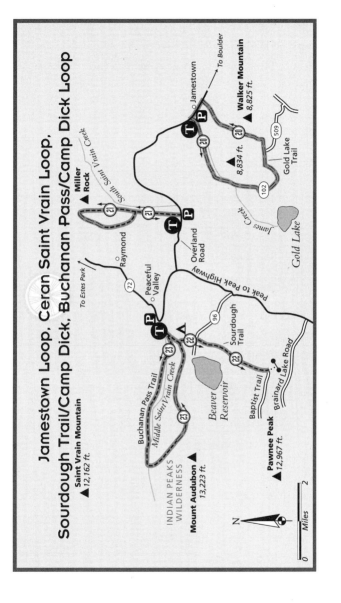

Land status: Private; Arapaho National Forest.

Map: Zia Design/Boulder County Mountain Bike map.

Access: From the intersection of Broadway and Canyon Road (Colorado Highway 119) in Boulder, drive or pedal 3.4 miles north on Broadway to Lee Hill Road. Follow Lee Hill Road to Old Stage Road, and go 4 miles to an intersection with Lefthand Canyon Road. Go left 2 miles and turn left on County Road 94 to Jamestown. Turn left on Ward Street. Park on the right.

The Ride

0.0 Pedal up Ward Street, which becomes a four-wheel-drive road.

0.6 Continue straight up the four-wheel-drive road. The grade steepens and the tread becomes rockier.

1.4 Bounce uphill on rocky tread (3+) where the stream has washed out the road.

1.6 Pass an abandoned mine on the right. Continue straight on smooth tread.

2.8 Another old mine on the right. Continue straight to an iron gate and James Creek.

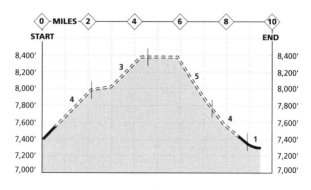

3.0 Go left to James Creek (which can be swift and dangerous during spring runoff) and pedal, paddle, swim, or wade across to the road on the other side. Continue up the main road, through a rocky (3) patch to an old road on the left.

3.3 Continue straight and up a strenuous, rutted-out track to the top of a ridge and catch your breath.

4.1 Go left at a three-way junction through a cut-over area.

4.6 Another three-way junction. Pedal left on Forest Road 509, up a short, steep, rocky pitch (4).

5.5 A road goes left; continue straight. Bomb down an intermittently rocky stretch to a three-way junction. Stop here to lower your seat, tighten those helmet straps, and reconsider that death and disability insurance you passed up last month. Now plunge into a wild downhill.

6.1 Go left, down a wickedly steep, rocky, dangerous, rutted-out (at least a 5) four-wheel-drive road to an abandoned mine on the right. Stop here if you need to regroup.

6.6 Continue down the rocky, rough road. Cross a stream and pedal past abandoned mining equipment and through a gate.

8.2 Everyone still in one piece? Go right, running fast down a maintained dirt road.

8.5 Welcome back to Jamestown. Go left on Main Street and past the Post Office to Ward Street.

9.5 Turn left to your car.

Ceran Saint Vrain Loop

Location: 18 miles northwest of Boulder. See map on page 77.

Distance: 5.9-mile loop.

Time: 1 to 2 hours.

Tread: 4.7 miles on singletrack and 1.2 miles on wide doubletrack.

Aerobic level: Moderate, with a few strenuous climbs.

Technical difficulty: 2 to 4 on singletrack; 2 to 3 on doubletrack.

Hazards: Watch for other trail users, especially during weekends. Ride in control—some singletrack sections are narrow with abrupt drop-offs above the river.

Highlights: Excellent singletrack along South Saint Vrain Creek. Climb to the top of Miller Rock for beautiful views. And all just a short drive from downtown Boulder. Bring your fishing rod.

Land status: Roosevelt National Forest.

Map: Zia Design/Boulder County Mountain Bike map.

Access: From the intersection of Broadway and Canyon Road (Colorado Highway 119) in Boulder, go 3.4 miles north on Broadway to Lee Hill Road. Follow Lee Hill Road to Old Stage Road, and go 4 miles to an intersection with Lefthand Canyon Road. Go left 2 miles to County Road 94 to Jamestown. Continue 4.7 miles to the entrance of Ceran

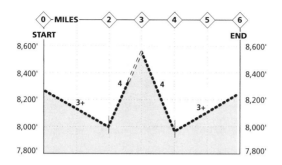

Saint Vrain Trail and turn right to the trailhead and parking. Total distance from Boulder to the trailhead is about 18 miles.

The Ride

0.0 From the parking lot pedal over a bridge to the start of the singletrack. Pedal along the beautiful South Saint Vrain Creek, scrambling over a short, rocky, technical section (4).

0.4 Continue along the river as the trail narrows. Beware of drop-offs on the right. As the trail leaves the river it begins a healthy descent.

1.9 Go left and uphill, fighting rocky tread.

2.1 Trail junction at the top of a hill. Go left up the short but strenuous hill.

2.4 Trail junction. Pedal right on tight singletrack.

2.7 Junction with a doubletrack ATV road. Pedal left on the doubletrack, up a short hill and over granite slickrock. Miller Rock is on the right.

2.9 Continue straight.

3.0 Trail junction. Go left and rip downhill on singletrack.

3.5 Go right for more fun downhill to the main trail.

4.0 Go right on the main trail, rolling up and down several quick hills and through cool pine forest.

5.9 Skitter across the bridge to the parking lot.

Sourdough Trail/ Camp Dick

Location: 32 miles northwest of Boulder, off Colorado Highway 72 (Peak to Peak Highway). See map on page 77.

Distance: 12.2 miles out and back.

Time: 2 to 3.5 hours.

Tread: 12.2 miles of excellent singletrack.

Aerobic level: Strenuous, with a stiff climb out of Camp Dick. This ride starts at 8,400 feet and tops out at 10,000 feet. Acclimate to these elevations before attempting this ride.

Technical difficulty: 2 to 4+ on singletrack, with some very rocky sections.

Hazards: Be prepared for sudden weather changes. Also, watch for root- and rock infested sections of trail.

Highlights: The best singletrack in Boulder County, offering challenges even to expert riders. A terrific summer ride through deep pine forest. Spectacular views east. Also see Ride 23.

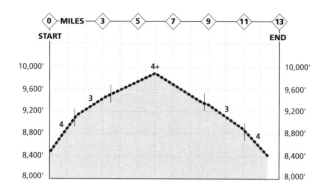

Land status: Roosevelt National Forest.

Map: Zia Design/Boulder County Mountain Bike map.

Access: From the intersection of Broadway and Canyon Road (Colorado Highway 119) in Boulder, drive 16 miles west on Canyon Road to Nederland. Turn right onto Colorado Highway 72 and drive 15 miles north to the Camp Dick turnoff on the left. Turn left and go 1 mile to the obvious trailhead on the left.

The Ride

0.0 Pedal up the smooth South Saint Vrain Trail.

0.3 The trail forks. Go right and gently climb.

0.7 Turn left onto Sourdough Trail, where the fun begins! Crank up a steep, rocky staircase (4+) to a ridge.

1.5 Zip downhill on smooth trail.

1.9 Cross a bridge over a small stream.

2.1 Lean right to stay on the trail and in a short distance go right again. Enjoy more downhill on smooth tread.

2.4 Cross Beaver Reservoir Road and continue on tight singletrack. Pedal through a burned area to the top of a hill.

3.1 Roll downhill, bunny hopping over some dead trees on smooth, sweet singletrack.

3.5 Cross another road and start a rocky climb (4+).

3.7 The trail forks. Follow the sign for Trail 835 on the right, up rocky singletrack (4).

4.4 Junction with Wapiti-Baptiste Trail. Continue on Sourdough Trail, climbing steadily.

5.4 Roll into a beautiful meadow with spectacular views of the Indian Peaks and a pond on the left. Follow rocky singletrack around the pond.

6.1 Junction with Baptist Trail on the right. Stop here and retrace your route back to the trailhead.

12.2 South Saint Vrain trailhead.

23

Buchanan Pass/ Camp Dick Loop

Location: 32 miles northwest of Boulder, off Colorado Highway 72 (Peak to Peak Highway). See map on page 77.

Distance: 11.5-mile loop.

Time: 2 to 3.5 hours.

Tread: 10.0 miles on singletrack and 1.5 miles on forest roads.

Aerobic level: Strenuous, with a number of technical sections. A high-elevation ride.

Technical difficulty: 2 on roads; 2 to 5+ on singletrack, with very rocky sections.

Hazards: Rocky Horror ride! Expect lots of rocky and root-bound technical tests uphill and down. Be prepared for sudden weather changes.

Highlights: A great singletrack challenge for advanced riders. Beautiful scenery along Middle Saint Vrain Creek, with occasional views to the Indian Peaks. Also see Ride 22.

Land status: Roosevelt National Forest. Check the trail status with the Forest Service.

Map: Zia Design/Boulder County Mountain Bike map.

Access: From the intersection of Broadway and Canyon Road (Colorado Highway 119) in Boulder, drive 16 miles west on Canyon Road to Nederland. Turn right onto Colorado Highway 72 and drive 15 miles north to the Camp

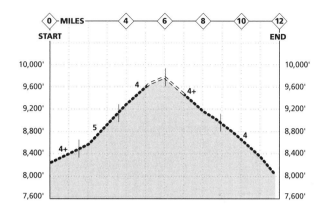

Dick turnoff on the left. Turn left and go 1 mile to the obvious trailhead on the left.

The Ride

0.0 Pedal west on the smooth South Saint Vrain Trail.

0.3 The trail forks. Go right and climb gradually.

0.7 Sourdough Trail goes left; continue straight on Buchanan Pass Trail.

0.8 The trail forks again. Go left up singletrack.

1.3 Cross Forest Road 507. Pedal over a bridge and go left up rocky, tight singletrack (5-) to smoother tread.

1.8 Pedal on smooth tread to a junction with a trail on the right.

2.1 Continue straight up a short, rocky (3+) hill to a smooth section of trail.

2.8 Push or pedal through a very rocky (5) section to the top of a small hill with huge rocks overlooking Timberline Falls on the left. This makes a great rest or lunch stop.

3.4   Crank up a short, rocky hill to smoother tread and a log bridge.

4.1   Pedal or push through a rock garden (a solid 5) to an open area with great views of the Indian Peaks.

4.6   Continue on tight singletrack (4) to Middle Saint Vrain Road.

5.2   Cross over a bridge and go left down the road.

5.4   Go right on Coney Flat Road (Forest Road 507), up a steep, rocky hill (4), to a fork in the road. Go left to a meadow with ponds.

6.1   Cross log bridges to Forest Road 507.

6.7   Where the road bends right, go straight on the marked hiker's trail, down a rocky hill to a small pond.

7.0   Pedal or walk past three small ponds, then up a short hill.

7.3   Crank down two technical (4+) downhills, then climb up a loose, rocky hill.

8.0   Turn left onto Forest Road 507.

8.6   The road forks. Go right on Forest Road 507.

9.4   Pedal over to a marked trail on the left (it's 25 feet off the road). Go right.

9.6   Go left on another trail featuring awesome singletrack. Fun, fun, and more fun from here to the finish.

9.8   The trail forks. Go right, down tight, technical singletrack (4). The trail negotiates steep steps and three small streams.

10.3   Trail junction. Go straight, down the rocky (4) Sourdough Trail.

10.8   Trail junction. Go right on the smooth Middle Saint Vrain Road to return to the trailhead.

11.5   Trailhead.

South Saint Vrain Loop

Location: 14 miles north of Nederland.

Distance: 9.8-mile loop.

Time: 2 to 4 hours.

Tread: 2.3 miles on doubletrack and 7.7 miles on single-track.

Aerobic level: Strenuous, with a lot of technical riding and climbing.

Technical difficulty: 2 to 5+.

Hazards: This ride is a bike and rider basher. The first half of the ride will rattle your teeth and test your ability to clear extended technical riding. Expect tough riding on tight singletrack with short, steep hills and prolonged technical stretches.

Highlights: For the expert rider only. Excellent technical riding on tight singletrack will demand your utmost attention. Staying on the bike the whole way is reserved for only a few exceptional cyclists. Don't let that keep you away from a great ride with a lot of technical riding.

Land status: Roosevelt National Forest.

Map: Trails Illustrated—Indian Peaks #103.

Access: From Boulder travel west on Canyon Road (Colorado Highway 119) to Nederland. From Nederland travel north on Colorado Highway 72 (Peak to Peak Highway) for 14.1 miles to County Road 96. Turn left on County Road 96

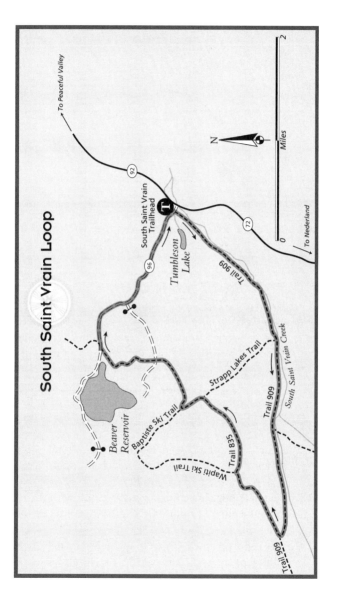

South Saint Vrain Loop

To Peaceful Valley

92

South Saint Vrain Trailhead

96

Tumbleson Lake

72

Beaver Reservoir

Baptiste Ski Trail

Wapiti Ski Trail

Trail 835

Strapp Lakes Trail

Trail 909

Trail 909

Trail 909

South Saint Vrain Creek

Trail 909

To Nederland

N

0   Miles   2

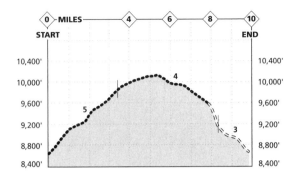

| 0 | MILES | 4 | 6 | 8 | 10 |

START   END

10,400'   10,400'
10,000'   10,000'
9,600'   9,600'
9,200'   9,200'
8,800'   8,800'
8,400'   8,400'

and cross over South Saint Vrain Creek to the trailhead for Trail 909 on the left. Park along the road. The ride starts here.

The Ride

0.0   Follow Trail 909 into the woods along the north side of South Saint Vrain Creek. There is very technical riding from the get-go. The trail climbs at a steady grade along the river through several technical, rocky (4) sections. If you are doing this ride during the summer months and have time to look down, enjoy beautiful wildflowers that bloom along the creek.

1.2   Reach a short, steep section up several steps. Beyond the steps the trail travels through a nice aspen forest and open meadow on good singletrack.

1.9   Reach Baptist Road and a gauging station on the left near the creek. Go right on Baptist Road up to a trail junction at a gate.

2.6   Go right on Trail 909. Things get very ugly here. Pedal, push, or be pushed up the very (5+) steep, technical rocky hill. The trail skirts private property and reaches Strapp Lakes Trail on the right.

2.8 Strapp Lakes Trail. Continue straight and down on Trail 909 to a junction with Sourdough Trail.

3.1 Sourdough Trail. Trails 909 and 835 share the same tread for over 0.5 mile of gradual, rocky, technical climbing, passing Red Rock Trail on the left. Keep those legs moving!

4.2 The trail splits. Go right on the Sourdough Trail 835, climbing up past Wapiti Ski Trail on the left.

4.9 Reach Wapiti Ski Trail junction. Continue straight on Sourdough Trail down into an open meadow with a small pond on the right. Look back to the west for spectacular views to the Indian Peaks. Continue past the pond and through the meadow where the trail veers to the left and drops steeply on rocky tread to a junction with Baptiste Ski Trail on the left.

6.5 Reach Baptiste Ski Trail on the left. Continue on Sourdough Trail down to a dirt road and trailhead.

7.9 Reach the Sourdough trailhead and a dirt road. Go right down the dirt road through an old burn area to County Road 96.

8.6 Go right on County Road 96 and back to the trailhead.

9.8 Back at the trailhead.

Sourdough Trail

Location: 7 miles east of Nederland on Colorado Highway 72 (Peak to Peak Highway).

Distance: 12.4 miles out and back.

Time: 1.5 to 2.5 hours.

Tread: 12.2 miles of excellent singletrack.

Aerobic level: Moderate, with a few steep climbs. This ride starts at 9,200 feet and tops out at 10,200 feet. Acclimate to elevation before attempting this ride.

Technical difficulty: 2 to 3+, with some very rocky sections.

Hazards: Be prepared for sudden weather changes; watch for roots and rocks on sections of trail.

Highlights: The best singletrack in Boulder County. A great summer ride through dense pine forest with occasional views of outstanding scenery to the east. Why overheat on the lower elevation trails when you can do the Sourdough? Also see Rides 22 and 23.

Land status: Roosevelt National Forest.

Map: Zia Design/Boulder County Mountain Bike map.

Access: From the intersection of Broadway and Canyon Road (Colorado Highway 119) in Boulder, drive 16 miles west up Canyon Road to the town of Nederland. Turn right onto Colorado Highway 72 and drive 7 miles north. Turn

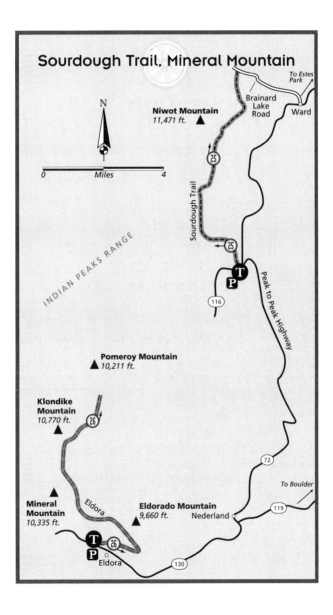

Sourdough Trail, Mineral Mountain

N

0   Miles   4

To Estes Park

Brainard Lake Road

Ward

Niwot Mountain
11,471 ft.

25

Sourdough Trail

25

T
P

116

Peak to Peak Highway

INDIAN PEAKS RANGE

Pomeroy Mountain
10,211 ft.

Klondike
Mountain
10,770 ft.

26

72

To Boulder

Mineral
Mountain
10,335 ft.

Eldora

Eldorado Mountain
9,660 ft.

Nederland

119

T
P

26

Eldora

130

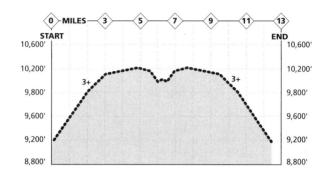

left onto County Road 116 (toward the University of Colorado Research Station) and go 0.5 mile to a parking area on the left and the trailhead on the right.

The Ride

0.0 From the parking area cross County Road 116 (watch for traffic) and pick up Sourdough Trail, which climbs gradually.

0.3 Cross a small bridge and continue to climb the rocky (3) singletrack to an open area with great views to the east.

0.8 Climb a series of tight, 3+ switchbacks to an open area with power lines.

1.4 Crank up rocky singletrack (3+) and descend to a short, rocky section (a solid 4).

1.7 Continue uphill.

1.8 Junction with a cross-country ski trail. Stay on the main trail as it climbs through a rocky section to the top of a small ridge.

2.4 Pedal down to a bridge crossing.

2.7 Cross the bridge and begin an extended climb through some tight switchbacks and rocky sections (3+) to an open area with great views.

3.9 Continue on beautiful singletrack that threads around stands of pine and along the edges of sun-struck meadows.

4.7 The trail skirts a small bog. Watch for a giant fallen tree across the trail. Bank left onto a user-created path to detour around the root wad. Back on the trail, crank up a short, rocky section (3+) to the top of a ridge.

5.3 Begin a sweet downhill to a junction with Little Raven Trail on the left.

5.7 Hang on for a steep, rocky section with steps.

6.1 Cross a bridge and pedal north.

6.2 The trail ends on paved Brainard Lake Road. Turn around and retrace your route to the Sourdough trailhead.

12.4 Look both ways for traffic before crossing County Road 116 to your car.

Mineral Mountain

Location: 20 miles west of Boulder, in the town of Eldora. See map on page 93.

Distance: 11.2 miles out and back.

Time: 2 to 3.5 hours.

Tread: 11.2 miles on four-wheel-drive roads.

Aerobic level: Strenuous, with some moderate sections.

Technical difficulty: 1 to 4.

Hazards: Watch for traffic on the route. Downhills are loose and rocky. Weather can change suddenly.

Highlights: An awesome hill climb, beautiful wildflowers, and panoramic views of the Indian Peaks from Caribou Flats.

Land status: Roosevelt National Forest.

Map: Zia Design/Boulder County Mountain Bike map.

Access: From the intersection of Broadway and Canyon Road (Colorado Highway 119) in Boulder, drive 16 miles west on Canyon Road to Nederland. Go left on Colorado Highway 72 (Peak to Peak Highway) and drive 1 mile south to County Road 130. Turn right at the sign to Eldora and drive 3 miles on County Road 130 to the intersection of Eldorado Avenue and 6th Street in Eldora. Mileage readings begin here.

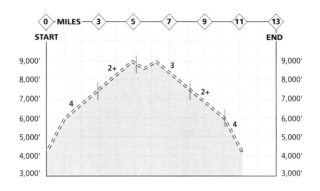

The Ride

0.0 From the corner of Eldorado Avenue and 6th Street, pedal east up 6th and go left on Washington Street. Pedal toward a cabin with elk horns on the front.

0.1 Go straight past the cabin and garage, where the road turns right. Continue straight as the road narrows and becomes rockier and steeper. Crank up rocky tread (3) to an easier grade.

0.4 Crank up more rocky tread (4) to an obvious flat area with great views east.

0.9 The grade eases for a short distance and the road cuts left.

1.2 Continue climbing through aspen forest. The road passes a small pond on the right.

1.4 The road winds around the pond, past beautiful wildflowers on the side of the hill, then switches back right.

1.7 Jam it up a short, steep, rocky section (3) to a hilltop.

2.0 Drop down a short hill. The road levels off and runs surprisingly smooth. Enjoy it—this doesn't last long.

2.4 Crank up another rocky, loose section. The grade eases.

2.7 Cruise for a short distance until—you guessed it—the grade steepens and the tread turns loose and rocky.

2.9 Gear down for a rocky climb (4), then spin onto an easier grade for a short distance. Legs feeling heavy?

3.4 A spur road goes left. Instead, go right up a steep, rocky hill that rates a 4 to a flat area.

3.7 All that climbing was worth it. Roll across the flats, past bristlecone pines and beautiful wildflowers in the foreground and a panoramic view of the Indian Peaks to the north.

4.5 A spur road goes left; continue straight.

4.7 Come to a three-way intersection. Go right on a smooth, flat road, then hang on where the road drops suddenly. It's steep, loose, and rocky.

5.6 Roll into the old Caribou townsite. Take a well-deserved rest and enjoy the scenery before retracing your route back to Eldora.

11.2 Cruise past the antlered cabin and pedal to your car.

Golden Gate
State Park Loop

Location: 14 miles northwest of Golden.

Distance: 8.2-mile loop.

Time: 2 to 3 hours.

Tread: 5.3 miles on singletrack and 2.9 miles on double-track.

Aerobic level: Moderate, with several strenuous climbs.

Technical difficulty: 2 to 3 on doubletrack; 2 to 4+ on singletrack.

Hazards: Loose rocks, downed trees, several stream crossings, and small drop-offs on the descent.

Highlights: Scenic views; challenging technical climbs and descents. This ride is not for the faint of heart.

Land status: Colorado State Park.

Map: Golden Gate State Park.

Access: From the intersection of U.S. Highway 6 and Colorado Highway 93 near Golden, drive 1.4 miles north on Colorado Highway 93 and turn left on Golden Gate Canyon Road. Go 12.3 miles to the Visitor Center and entrance to Golden Gate State Park ($3.00 for a day pass). Turn right on Ralston Creek Road and go 1.9 miles to the Bridge Creek trailhead and parking lot. From the intersection of Broadway and Baseline Road in Boulder, go 19 miles

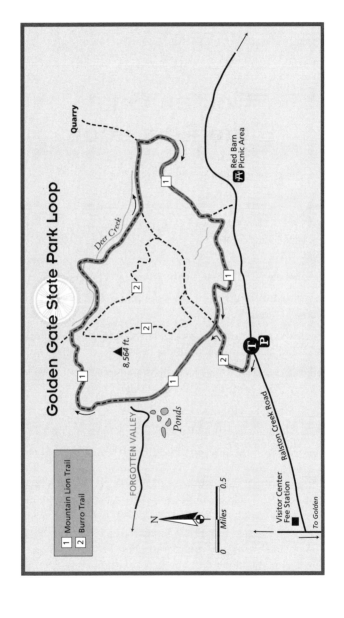

Golden Gate State Park Loop

Quarry

Deer Creek

8,564 ft.

FORGOTTEN VALLEY

Ponds

Red Barn Picnic Area

1 Mountain Lion Trail
2 Burro Trail

N

Miles

0   0.5

Visitor Center Fee Station

Ralston Creek Road

To Golden

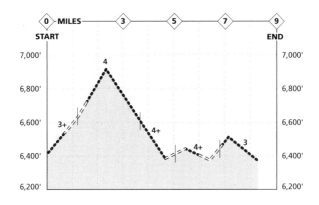

south on Colorado Highway 93 to Golden Gate Canyon Road. Turn right and follow directions above.

The Ride

0.0 From the parking lot cross the bridge over Ralston Creek and go left on Burro Trail. Climb steeply up rocky singletrack (4-) to the top of a small ridge.

0.6 Bear left onto the doubletrack Mountain Lion Trail. Descend to an abandoned settlement and a pond, then climb washed-out doubletrack.

1.5 Junction with Buffalo Trail. Continue straight on Mountain Lion Trail, which turns to singletrack. Climb a set of steep switchbacks to a notch below Windy Peak.

2.3 Continue on Mountain Lion Trail, descending on tight, rocky singletrack through dense pine forest.

2.5 Junction with Burro Trail. Go left on Mountain Lion Trail, which becomes rockier and steeper with tight switchbacks. Watch for drops over ledges (4+).

2.9 The trail now winds along Deer Creek, crossing the creek several times on old tree bridges. Cruise down open singletrack.

4.7 Junction with Quarry Trail. Turn right on Mountain Lion Trail, crossing a bridge. Then begin a gradual climb on open doubletrack.

5.4 Turn left on Mountain Lion Trail, now singletrack, for a steep descent to the Nott Creek trailhead.

5.9 Go right past the bathrooms staying on the Mountain Lion Trail. Drop down a short hill, then resume climbing steadily on soft singletrack. Grunt through a series of switchbacks to a short downhill.

7.2 Pedal right to stay on Mountain Lion Trail.

7.7 Go left on Burro Trail, descending swiftly to Ralston Creek.

8.2 Cross the bridge and you're home free.

White Ranch Loop

Location: 17 miles south of Boulder, on Colorado Highway 93.

Distance: 14.6-mile loop.

Time: 2 to 3.5 hours.

Tread: 6.6 miles on doubletrack and 8.0 miles on singletrack.

Aerobic level: Strenuous, with several long climbs.

Technical difficulty: 2 to 4 on doubletrack; 2 to 5+ on singletrack.

Hazards: Rocky sections with bad landings; steep steps on tight singletrack. Watch for other riders and trail users on this popular trail. Beginners should stay away from this ride.

Highlights: Excellent singletrack, close to Boulder and Denver, with great views of the Front Range. Numerous spur trails and doubletrack roads offer extra riding miles.

Land status: Jefferson County Open Space.

Map: Jefferson County Open Space: White Ranch.

Access: From the intersection of Broadway and Baseline Road in Boulder, go 17 miles south on Colorado Highway 93 (Broadway) to White Ranch Road. Turn right and follow signs to the parking lot. From the intersection of U.S. Highway 6 and Colorado Highway 93 near Golden, drive 3.4

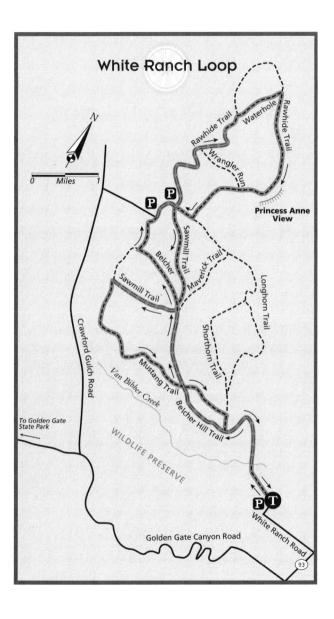

White Ranch Loop

N

0 ——— Miles ——— 1

Rawhide Trail

Waterhole

Rawhide Trail

Wrangler Run

Princess Anne View

P P

Sawmill Trail

Belcher

Sawmill Trail

Maverick Trail

Longhorn Trail

Shorthorn Trail

Mustang Trail

Belcher Hill Trail

Van Bibber Creek

Crawford Gulch Road

To Golden Gate State Park

WILDLIFE PRESERVE

P T

White Ranch Road

Golden Gate Canyon Road

93

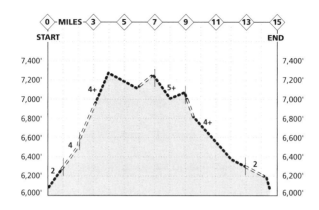

miles north on Colorado Highway 93 and turn left on White Ranch Road. Follow signs to the parking lot.

The Ride

0.0 From the parking lot pedal onto Belcher Hill Trail. Go down a short rocky section (3), then up over water bars to a set of steep steps and a bridge.

0.7 Cross the bridge and begin an extended climb up Belcher Hill Trail. Crank up a loose, rocky section.

1.8 Longhorn Trail goes right; instead, continue straight on loose, rocky tread (4).

2.5 The grade mellows to a junction with Mustang Trail. Continue straight on wide doubletrack tread.

3.0 Junction with Sawmill Trail. Go straight up the well-marked Belcher Hill Trail, now singletrack, over a series of steep water bars. Pedal to an open area with great views of the foothills. Roll along tight singletrack.

3.8 Mustang Trail comes in on the left. Instead, go right and drop down a series of water bars (3+) to the upper parking lot.

4.2 Cross the parking lot to an obvious trail on the north end. Drop over several water bars and onto Rawhide Trail.

4.6 Pedal left on the wide Rawhide Trail (Wrangler Run goes right).

5.4 Continue straight up a short, steep hill.

6.4 Rawhide Trail goes left. Instead, go straight on Waterhole Trail.

6.5 Join the Rawhide Trail again where it turns to singletrack. Crank up a rocky 4+ section to the Princess Anne View.

7.2 Continue on awesome singletrack to extremely steep, rocky steps—a solid 5+, even if you're a trials rider. Most people dismount here and hike down the steps.

7.9 Wrangler Run comes in on the right. Go left on Rawhide Trail, up a steep hill and over more water bars (4+).

8.2 Pedal right on Longhorn Trail to the parking lot.

8.6 Cross the parking area to Sawmill Trail. Pedal straight on this sweet singletrack.

9.3 At a junction with Belcher Hill Trail, go straight on the wide Sawmill Trail, past several campsites. Crank uphill, then fly down tight singletrack.

10.0 Turn left on Mustang Trail, down steep steps (4) to a small stream. Then cruise along wonderful singletrack.

11.9 Junction with Belcher Hill Trail. Go straight on the Mustang Trail, bouncing over a set of highly technical (5-), steep steps.

12.5 Lean right onto Longhorn Trail, down a loose, rocky (4) section.

12.7 Go left on Belcher Hill Trail, down a steep hill. (CAUTION: Watch for other trail users.)

13.9 Cross a bridge and continue on singletrack to the trailhead.

14.6 Cruise into the parking lot.

Green Mountain Park Loop

Location: 8 miles west of Denver, in the town of Lakewood.

Distance: 6.8-mile loop.

Time: 1 to 2 hours.

Tread: 1.9 miles on doubletrack and 4.9 miles on singletrack.

Aerobic level: Moderate, with one long, steep climb.

Technical difficulty: 1 to 2 on doubletrack; 2 to 3 on singletrack.

Hazards: Watch your speed on the downhill; yield to other trail users.

Highlights: This loop can be ridden almost year-round. It offers an excellent workout and good singletrack for the novice looking to improve. Also see Ride 30.

Land status: Jefferson County Open Space.

Map: Jefferson County Open Space. Green Mountain.

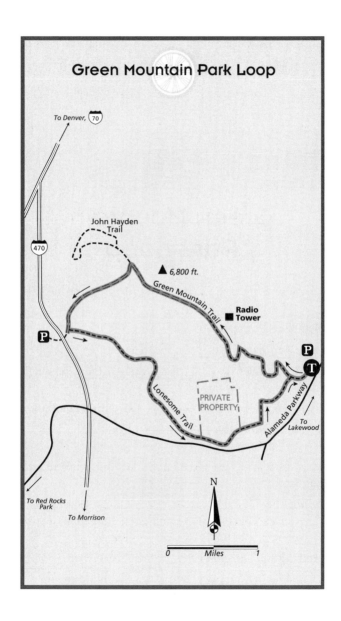

Green Mountain Park Loop

To Denver, 70

470

John Hayden Trail

▲ 6,800 ft.

Green Mountain Trail

Radio Tower

P

P

T

Lonesome Trail

PRIVATE PROPERTY

Alameda Parkway

To Lakewood

To Red Rocks Park

To Morrison

N

0   Miles   1

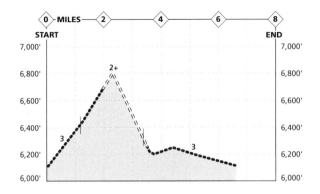

Access: From I–25 in Denver, go 7 miles west on U.S. Highway 6 to the Simms Street/Union Street Exit. Turn left on South Union Street and go 1.8 miles. Turn right onto Alameda Parkway and go 1.5 miles to a trailhead parking area on the right.

The Ride

0.0 From the parking area pedal up a short hill, then roll downhill.

0.2 Four-way intersection. Go right and start climbing a steep hill on good singletrack. Pedal over some rocky sections (3) to an intersection with an old service road.

1.7 Go left on the service road and up a short hill to the high point of the ride.

2.3 Continue on the service road, picking up speed as the road plunges down toward Colorado Highway 470.

3.7 Just before the intersection with the C–470 bike path, go left onto smooth, hardpack singletrack (Lonesome Trail).

4.6 Cross an intersection, staying on the singletrack, and climb a short but steep rocky pitch to the crest of a small hill.

4.8 Continue on singletrack as it curves around the south side of Green Mountain.

6.7 Climb a short hill.

6.8 Turn right into the parking lot.

Dakota Ridge and Matthews/Winters Park Loop

Location: 10 miles west of Denver.

Distance: 6.5-mile loop.

Time: 1 to 2 hours.

Tread: 0.5 mile on paved road, 1.1 miles on doubletrack, and 4.9 miles on singletrack.

Aerobic level: Moderate, but with several steep, strenuous climbs.

Technical difficulty: 1 on paved road; 2 to 3 on doubletrack; 3 to 4+ on singletrack.

Hazards: Watch for traffic when crossing the highway. Several rocky sections on Dakota Ridge.

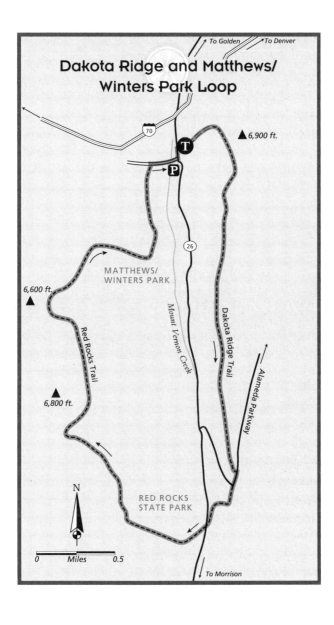

Dakota Ridge and Matthews/
Winters Park Loop

To Golden   To Denver

I-70

T

P

▲ 6,900 ft.

26

MATTHEWS/
WINTERS PARK

6,600 ft.
▲

Red Rocks Trail

Mount Vernon Creek

Dakota Ridge Trail

Alameda Parkway

▲
6,800 ft.

N

RED ROCKS
STATE PARK

0   Miles   0.5

To Morrison

Highlights: Technical singletrack on Dakota Ridge; frequent dips and fast singletrack on Matthews/Winters section. Also see Ride 29.

Land status: Jefferson County Open Space.

Map: Jefferson County Open Space.

Access: From Denver drive west on I–70 to the Morrison/Golden interchange (Colorado Highway 26). Go 0.25 mile south on Colorado Highway 26 to the entrance of Matthews/Winters Park.

The Ride

0.0 From the parking lot pedal east, across Colorado Highway 26 (CAUTION: Watch for traffic), and climb the obvious doubletrack up the steep hill.

0.8 Turn right on singletrack to gain the ridge and stay on singletrack through some tough (5), rocky sections. Then drop down to Alameda Parkway, dismounting to walk rough sections as needed. There are at least four technical test pieces rated 4 or

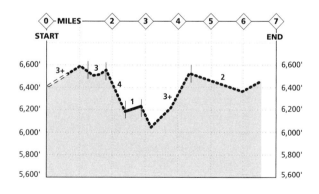

above that require expert bike handling skills on this descent.

2.4 Cross Alameda Parkway and head south to Red Rocks Trail. Follow the trail up a short, steep, rocky (3+) section to the ridge, then continue down fast singletrack to Morrison Road. Cross the road (CAUTION: Watch for traffic) and go through the entrance to Red Rocks Park.

3.2 Turn right onto Red Rocks Trail again and climb a steep hill with water bars (3+) to an intersection with Morrison Slide Trail.

4.2 Turn right to stay on Red Rocks Trail. Follow this fast singletrack to Village Walk Trail.

5.8 Go right on Village Walk Trail for a fast descent to the parking lot.

6.5 Cruise into the parking lot.

Chimney Gulch

Location: Golden.

Distance: 7.0 miles out and back.

Time: 1 to 2.5 hours.

Tread: 7.0 miles on singletrack.

Aerobic level: Strenuous, with a big climb up to Lookout Mountain Nature Center.

Technical difficulty: 4.

Hazards: A popular trail with hikers and mountain bikers. Be on the lookout for falling hang gliders.

Highlights: Chimney Gulch has seen a fair amount of trail work, and sections of the trail have been relocated. The trail is now a little friendlier for mountain bikers. The climb is still hard and technical and will require strong legs and lungs.

Land status: Jefferson County Open Space.

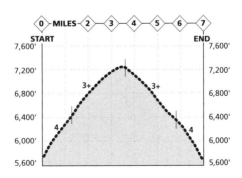

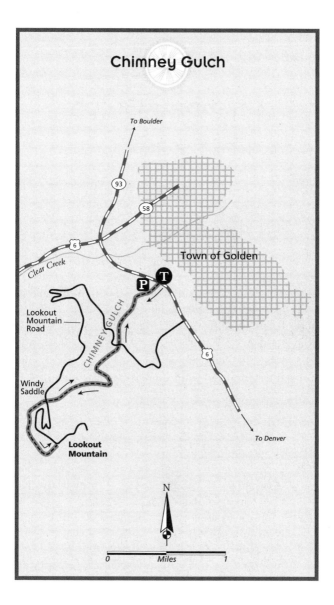

Chimney Gulch

To Boulder

93

58

6

Clear Creek

P **T**

Lookout
Mountain
Road

CHIMNEY GULCH

Town of Golden

6

Windy
Saddle

**Lookout
Mountain**

To Denver

N

0   *Miles*   1

Maps: USGS Golden/Morrison.

Access: From Denver travel west on U.S. Highway 6 to Golden. The parking area is located on the left just before a large TOWN OF GOLDEN sign and a wind sock (used by hang gliders); the ride starts here.

The Ride

0.0 From the parking area at the wind sock, travel across the open meadow to a doubletrack trail. Go left on the doubletrack up past a cement ditch. Go right on the singletrack trail and climb on tight tread up to the crest of a hill. Reach the top of the hill and begin to climb on tight singletrack up Chimney Gulch.

0.5 The trail narrows and passes by a small drainage and nice cottonwoods.

0.6 Begin climbing up past five steep switchbacks (4).

0.7 Go left on a private driveway and make a quick right on tight singletrack. Climb to Lariat Loop Road.

0.9 Cross Lariat Loop Road and follow tight, rocky singletrack up Chimney Gulch.

1.2 Extremely rocky terrain (4).

1.6 The gulch becomes narrow. Continue climbing up to a wooden footbridge.

1.8 Cross the footbridge and head into a beautiful stand of ponderosas. Very scenic riding through this section. Climb up to a second footbridge.

2.2 Cross over the second footbridge and climb on good tread up to Windy Saddle.

2.4 Cross the road and follow Beaver Brook Trail back into the woods. Excellent singletrack riding brings you to a trail junction.

2.6   Go left on Lookout Mountain Trail on steep, rocky tread through evergreens.

2.9   Reach an overlook and views to Clear Creek Canyon. The trail mellows out and reaches Colorow Road and the Lookout Mountain Nature Center across the road. Check out the nature center if you have the time. Keep your speed in check on the fast downhill and yield to uphill hikers and cyclists.

3.5   Lookout Mountain Nature Center. Turn around and retrace your route back to the trailhead.

7.0   Back at the trailhead.

Apex Park Loop

Location: 10 miles west of Denver.

Distance: 5.4-mile loop.

Time: 1 to 3 hours.

Tread: 0.3 mile on paved roads, 0.5 mile on doubletrack, and 4.6 miles on singletrack.

Aerobic level: Mostly moderate, with several strenuous climbs.

Technical difficulty: 1 on paved road; 2 on doubletrack; 3 to 4 on singletrack.

Hazards: Be alert for horseback riders and other trail users. Singletrack has tight turns and rocky sections.

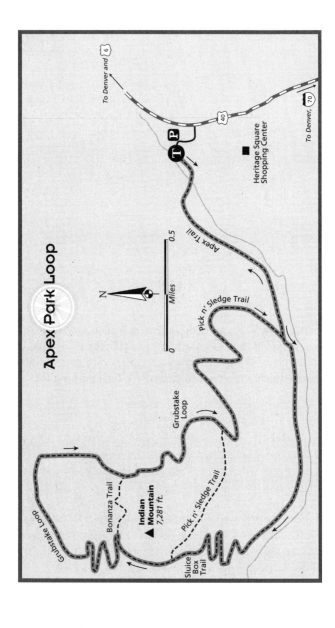

Apex Park Loop

N

Miles
0   0.5

To Denver and 6

40

To Denver, 70

P

T

Heritage Square
Shopping Center

Apex Trail

Pick n' Sledge Trail

Grubstake Loop

Grubstake Loop

Bonanza Trail

▲ Indian
Mountain
7,281 ft.

Pick n' Sledge Trail

Sluice Box Trail

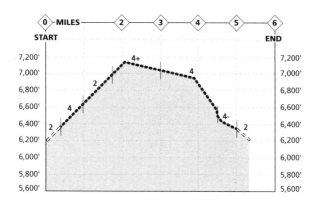

Highlights: Awesome singletrack; close to Denver; excellent, steep climbing with great views of Denver and the Front Range.

Land status: Jefferson County Open Space.

Map: Apex Park Open Space.

Access: From Denver take I–70 west to the Morrison exit (U.S. Highway 40). Go 1 mile north on U.S. Highway 40 to the Heritage Square entrance. Turn left toward Golden and make a quick left turn into Apex Park East parking lot.

The Ride

0.0 From the trailhead go west on Apex Trail.

0.7 Pedal past Pick n' Sledge Trail, over some water bars and rocky sections (4) to a junction with Sluice Box Trail.

1.4 Go right on Sluice Box Trail up some tight and rocky switchbacks (a solid 4) to Grubstake Loop.

2.3 Continue on Grubstake Loop to the top of Indian Mountain. Drop downhill on sweet singletrack, past

Bonanza Trail, and resume climbing on a short, steep section with water bars and rocks (4+ moves) to Pick n' Sledge Trail.

3.7 Swing down Pick n' Sledge Trail's steep, rocky descent to Apex Trail. Ride in control and anticipate several tight, rocky (4) sections with steep drop-offs.

4.6 Go left (east) on Apex Trail, over some rocky sections, to an open area.

5.4 Cross a bridge and roll into the parking lot.

33

Mount Falcon Park Loop

Location: 1.5 miles west of Morrison.

Distance: 9.5-mile loop.

Time: 1.5 to 3 hours.

Tread: 1.2 miles on doubletrack and 8.3 miles on singletrack.

Aerobic level: Strenuous, with a 1,400-foot elevation gain in the first 2.7 miles.

Technical difficulty: 1 to 2 on doubletrack; 3 to 4 on singletrack.

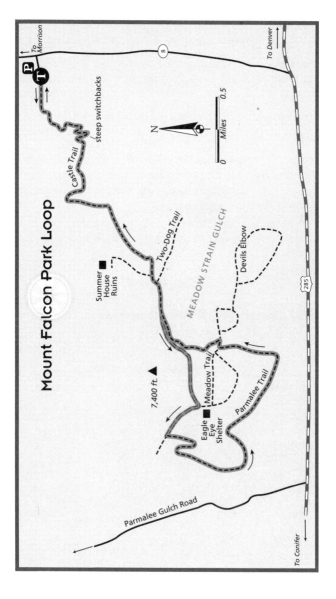

Mount Falcon Park Loop

N

0   0.5
Miles

To Morrison

P
T

steep switchbacks

Castle Trail

Two-Dog Trail

Summer House Ruins

MEADOW STRAIN GULCH

Devils Elbow

7,400 ft.

Meadow Trail

Eagle Eye Shelter

Parmalee Trail

Parmalee Gulch Road

To Denver

285

To Conifer

8

Hazards: Watch for horse-, foot-, and bike traffic. Slow down for water bars and tight turns on the downhill.

Highlights: Awesome uphill, great views of Red Rocks and Denver. This is some of the best singletrack in the Denver–Boulder area.

Land status: Jefferson County Open Space.

Map: Jefferson County Open Space.

Access: From Denver drive west on I–70 to the Golden/ Morrison Exit. Go 4 miles south on Colorado Highway 26 to Morrison. Turn right (west) on Main Street, then turn left on Colorado Highway 8 and drive 1.5 miles. Turn right onto Forest Avenue and follow signs to the trailhead. Total distance from Denver to the trailhead is 20 miles.

The Ride

0.0 The trail begins with a short downhill, then climbs steeply on good singletrack.

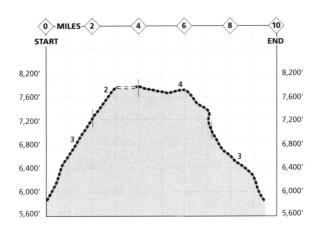

0.7	Continue to climb, looking straight ahead for great views of Red Rocks.
1.7	Continue to climb the steep hill. This is a good spot to stop for excellent views of Morrison and Denver.
2.3	Crank up a short, steep (3+) section and continue climbing to a saddle.
2.7	Take a well-deserved rest. You've just climbed 1,400 feet in the last 2.7 miles. Bear left on Castle Trail to a three-way intersection.
3.0	Continue straight on Castle Trail.
3.4	Make a right turn at another three-way intersection for a short downhill.
3.7	Pass bathrooms on the right and make a quick left-hand turn to Parmalee Trail. Follow this great, narrow singletrack (with a few sections rating a 4) to an intersection with Meadow Trail.
6.0	Turn right onto Meadow Trail.
6.1	Turn left and continue on Meadow Trail.
6.4	Turn right onto Castle Trail for a quick descent to the parking lot. Control your speed on the downhill—watch for tight turns and other trail users.
9.5	Back at the parking area and those cold liquids stashed in the cooler.

Reynolds Park Loop

Location: 40 miles southwest of Denver; 6 miles south of Conifer.

Distance: 5.3-mile loop.

Time: This route has been closed to bicycles, but it is a great place to hike. Just beware that the trail starts out steep!

Aerobic level: Moderate, with two big strenuous hills.

Technical difficulty: If mountain biking, it would have been 1 to 2 on doubletrack; 2 to 4- on singletrack.

Hazards: Watch for traffic on County Road 97. Smooth singletrack has intervals of rough, rocky sections.

Highlights: Great views of the South Platte area, excellent singletrack.

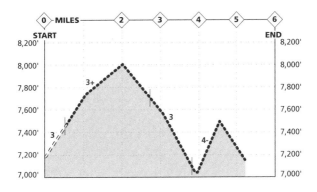

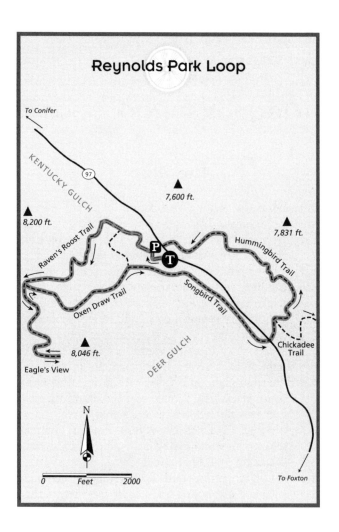

Reynolds Park Loop

To Conifer

KENTUCKY GULCH

97

▲
7,600 ft.

▲
8,200 ft.

▲
7,831 ft.

Raven's Roost Trail

P

T

Hummingbird Trail

Oxen Draw Trail

Songbird Trail

▲
8,046 ft.

DEER GULCH

Chickadee Trail

Eagle's View

N

0   Feet   2000

To Foxton

Land status: Jefferson County Open Space.

Map: Jefferson County Open Space.

Access: From Denver drive 25 miles west on U.S. Highway 285, through the town of Conifer. Turn left on Foxton Road (County Road 97) and go 5.2 miles to the Reynolds Park parking lot on the right.

The Ride

0.0 From the parking lot hike up and right, past the bathrooms to Elkhorn Trail.

0.1 Turn right on Elkhorn Trail. Climb up the tight singletrack as it switchbacks steeply uphill.

0.4 Turn right onto Raven's Roost Trail. Continue climbing on doubletrack, which turns to singletrack.

1.0 Turn left on Raven's Roost Trail. Descend to a small creek crossing.

1.3 Junction with Eagle's View/Oxen Draw Trails. Go right on Eagle's View Trail and climb steadily.

2.0 The trail ends on a ridge with great views of the South Platte area. Turn around and head back down to the trail junction at mile 1.3 above.

2.7 Go right on Oxen Draw Trail, crossing a stream several times and hiking over some rocky sections.

3.3 Bear right on Elkhorn Trail.

3.5 Go right on Songbird Trail, following along the stream. Cross a bridge and enter the lower parking area.

4.0 Cross the road and pick up Hummingbird Trail as it climbs steeply past Chickadee Trail. Continue climbing through tight switchbacks to an open ridge.

4.7 Watch your footing as Hummingbird Trail drops steeply to the road.

5.3 Cross the road to the parking lot and your car.

Waterton Canyon Loop

Location: 14 miles southwest of Denver.

Distance: 17.1 miles out and back.

Time: 2 to 3 hours.

Tread: 12.2 miles on doubletrack and gravel roads and 4.9 miles on singletrack.

Aerobic level: Mostly moderate, with a few strenuous climbs.

Technical difficulty: 1 on gravel road; 3 to 4 on singletrack; 2 on doubletrack.

Hazards: Watch for other travelers on the gravel road.

Highlights: Great singletrack. Bring your fishing rod; also an excellent area to view bighorn sheep.

Land status: Pike National Forest, Denver Water Board.

Maps: Trails Illustrated—Deckers/Rampart Range; Pike National Forest.

Access: From Denver drive south on I–25 to exit 194. Go west on Colorado Highway 470 to Colorado Highway 121 (Wadsworth Boulevard), then drive 4.1 miles south on

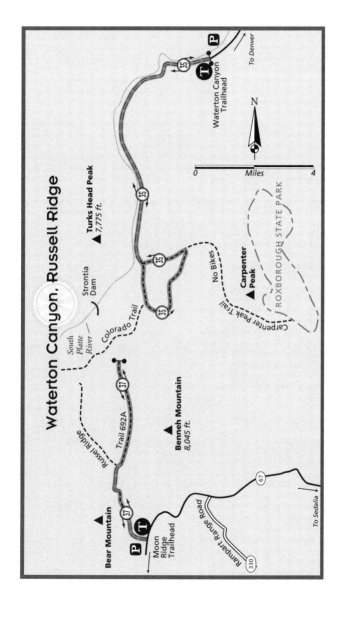

Waterton Canyon, Russell Ridge

Turks Head Peak ▲ 7,775 ft.

Strontia Dam

South Platte River

Colorado Trail

P **T** Waterton Canyon Trailhead

To Denver

N

0 — Miles — 4

No Bikes

Carpenter Peak Trail

Carpenter Peak ▲

ROXBOROUGH STATE PARK

Russel Ridge

Trail 692A

Benneh Mountain 8,045 ft.

Bear Mountain ▲

P **T** Moon Ridge Trailhead

Rampart Range Road

To Sedalia

67

330

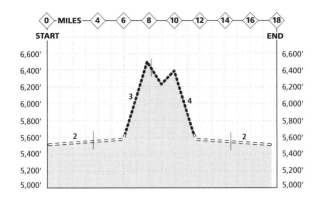

Colorado Highway 121 to the Waterton Canyon entrance. Turn left into the large parking lot. Total distance from Denver to trailhead is 14 miles.

The Ride

0.0 From the parking area pedal west across the road, past the Kaiser Water Treatment Plant, to the Waterton Canyon trailhead.

0.3 Pedal up the gravel road, along the beautiful South Platte River, past Strontia Dam to a junction with Colorado Trail, which joins in from the right.

6.6 Follow Colorado Trail on doubletrack, which dwindles to singletrack.

6.7 Continue on Colorado Trail, now climbing on beautiful singletrack, through a shaded pine forest. The trail switchbacks (3) to the top of a ridge and joins Carpenter Peak Trail.

7.8 Go left on Carpenter Pike Trail, climbing steeply on soft singletrack to a descent through dense pine forest.

8.7   Drop down the soft singletrack and pedal along a creek, crossing it twice.

9.2   Climb up tight singletrack to the top of a small ridge, then descend down the curving trail to a junction with an unnamed trail.

10.2   Turn left, still descending on tight singletrack. The trail becomes rocky and technical (a solid 4) for a short stretch before meeting Waterton Canyon Trail.

11.1   Turn right on the road and crank downhill, retracing your earlier route along the South Platte.

17.1   Cross the road and spin into the parking lot.

Deer Creek Canyon Park

Location: 12 miles southwest of Denver.

Distance: 7.6 miles out and back.

Time: 1 to 2 hours.

Tread: 5.1 miles on doubletrack and 2.5 miles on singletrack.

Aerobic level: Moderate, with a few steep sections.

Technical difficulty: 2 to 3 on doubletrack; 2 to 3 on singletrack.

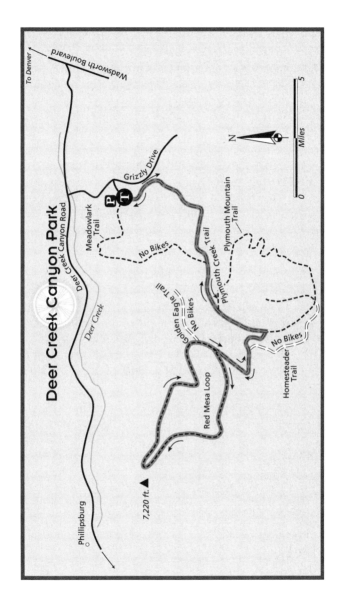

Deer Creek Canyon Park

To Denver

Wadsworth Boulevard

Deer Creek Canyon Road

Deer Creek

Phillipsburg

7,220 ft. ▲

Red Mesa Loop

Golden Eagle Trail

No Bikes

Meadowlark Trail

Grizzly Drive

P T

No Bikes

Plymouth Creek Trail

Plymouth Mountain Trail

No Bikes

Homesteader Trail

N

0   Miles   5

Hazards: Watch for other trail users. Fast downhill on singletrack has intervals of rough, rocky sections.

Highlights: A great workout close to Denver, with spectacular views of Denver and the Hogback Ridges.

Land status: Jefferson County Open Space.

Map: Jefferson County Open Space.

Access: From Denver take I–70 west to Colorado Highway 470 east. Exit onto Wadsworth Boulevard (Colorado Highway 121), and go 300 yards south on Wadsworth Boulevard to Deer Creek Canyon Road. Turn right (west) on Deer Creek Canyon Road and drive 4.9 miles to Grizzly Drive. Turn left and go 0.5 mile to the park entrance.

The Ride

0.0 From the parking area pedal west toward the bathrooms. Go left onto Plymouth Creek Trail and climb steadily up this sometimes rough and rocky trail.

1.1 At a junction with Meadowlark Trail, go straight on Plymouth Creek Trail. Grind through a short, steep,

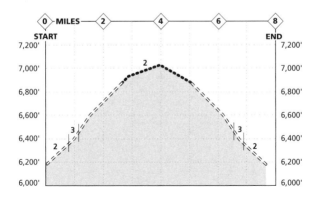

rocky section (3), then catch your breath and continue to climb to a junction with Plymouth Mountain Trail.

1.9   Go right, staying on Plymouth Creek Trail.

2.0   Homesteader Trail comes in from the left. Continue climbing as the grade eases to a junction with Red Mesa Loop.

2.5   Stop and enjoy the views of Denver and the plains to the east, then go left on Red Mesa Loop. The trail continues to climb gently, then turns to singletrack. Here's where the fun begins.

4.0   Take in the spectacular views and plunge down awesome, curving singletrack to the junction with Plymouth Creek Trail.

5.1   Oh boy, the joy of downhill! Continue down Plymouth Creek Trail, but watch for tight turns and anticipate meeting other trail users. Ride in control.

7.6   Pedal to the trailhead.

Russell Ridge

Location: 14 miles west of Sedalia on Colorado Highway 67. See map on page 128.

Distance: 10.0 miles out and back.

Time: 1.5 to 2.5 hours.

Tread: 1.8 miles on ATV trails, 2.2 miles on doubletrack, and 6.0 miles on wide singletrack.

Aerobic level: Mostly moderate; the first mile is the most strenuous.

Technical difficulty: 2 to 3.

Hazards: ATV traffic on weekends; dips and bumps on the descent to parking area.

Highlights: Great downhill, wonderful views of Devils Head and Pike National Forest.

Land status: Private, Columbine Bowmen; Pike National Forest.

Maps: Pike National Forest; Trails Illustrated—Deckers/Rampart Range.

Access: From I–25 in Denver, take exit 207 to U.S. Highway 85 and drive 20 miles south to Sedalia. Turn right on Colorado Highway 67 and drive 14 miles to the small village of Sprucewood. Turn right on County Road 40 just past the only store in town, go 100 yards, and turn right into a large dirt parking area.

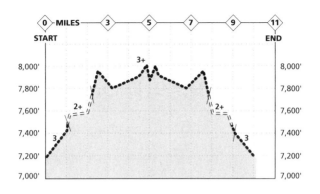

The Ride

0.0 From the parking area pedal up the obvious ATV trail. The first 200 yards are the steepest and you may have to walk your bike. Remember, what goes up must come down, and this downhill is a great way to end the ride.

0.9 Once you top out on the hill, look for singletrack on the other side of a fence post. Take this singletrack to the top of a small hill. This is private property that belongs to the Columbine Bowmen, so please stay on the designated trail. Go downhill, through a gate, to a four-way intersection.

1.5 Go straight on the main road, which continues downhill. Then chug up a short climb, past a yellow metal sign, to a three-way intersection.

2.3 Go right on Trail 692A and go up a short hill, then down past two trails on the right to the obvious power line.

3.4 This is the best part of the trail. Continue to climb along the ridgeline, enjoying great views, to a high point on the ridge.

4.8 Roll briefly downhill as the trail re-enters the forest.

5.0 Stop here and go left to a small cliff with outstanding views of the South Platte. Retrace your tracks to return to the trailhead. Good views of Devils Head.

10.0 Drop into the parking area.

Buck Gulch Trail Loop

Location: 30 miles southwest of Denver, in the South Platte Valley.

Distance: 10.4-mile loop.

Time: 1.5 to 3 hours.

Tread: 4.4 miles on doubletrack and 6.0 miles on single-track.

Aerobic level: Moderate, with several strenuous climbs (the trail gains 1,200 feet in the first 3 miles).

Technical difficulty: 2 to 3.

Hazards: Watch for pea gravel and sandy areas on the fast downhills.

Highlights: One of my favorite rides, featuring great climbs, awesome downhill, and well-groomed singletrack. This is just a great all-around ride. The downhill back to Pine Valley Ranch is fast and steep. Watch your speed and be on the lookout for other trail users. The ride has

Buck Gulch Trail Loop

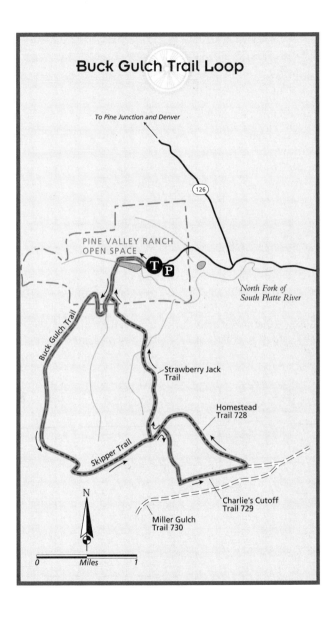

To Pine Junction and Denver

126

PINE VALLEY RANCH
OPEN SPACE

T P

North Fork of
South Platte River

Buck Gulch Trail

Strawberry Jack
Trail

Homestead
Trail 728

Skipper Trail

Charlie's Cutoff
Trail 729

Miller Gulch
Trail 730

N

0   Miles   1

changed somewhat due to the High Meadow fire of 1997. Also see rides 39, 40, 41, and 42.

Land status: Jefferson County Open Space, Pike National Forest.

Maps: Jefferson County Open Space; Pike National Forest.

Access: From I–25 in Denver go 25 miles west on U.S. Highway 285 (Hampden Avenue) to Pine Junction. Turn left on County Road 126 and go 5.9 miles. Turn right into the entrance of Pine Valley Ranch and park in the lower parking lot.

The Ride

0.0 From the lower parking lot pedal down to Narrow Gauge Trail. Follow Narrow Gauge Trail along the river to North Fork View Trail.

0.3 Go left on North Fork View Trail across the river to Buck Gulch Trail

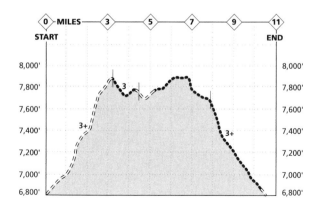

0.4 Turn onto Buck Gulch Trail and begin climbing, past Strawberry Jack Trail on the left, and switchbacking up into Buck Gulch.

0.8 Turn right onto some steep switchbacks with patches of loose gravel. Grunt up what seems to be a never-ending hill. Continue climbing on doubletrack to the junction with Skipper Trail, a national forest kiosk, and the end of the climbing for now.

3.2 Go left on Skipper Trail and let 'er rip on a wonderful downhill singletrack run.

4.0 Cross a small bridge and climb a short but steep pitch out of Buck Gulch.

4.5 Four-way intersection. Go right and uphill on an old logging road (Homestead Trail 728) to the top of a small hill.

5.0 Go left on Charlie's Cutoff Trail 729, rollicking over a swatch of slickrock (a good place for fat tire doodling). Then enjoy sweet, tight singletrack—great riding!

6.4 Turn left onto Homestead Trail 728 and pedal through a flat area with huge boulders on the right. Climb narrow singletrack to a saddle, then cruise down more, tight singletrack.

8.0 Four-way intersection. Go right on the tight Strawberry Jack Trail. Begin an exciting downhill run to Park View Trail. This section is so sweet.

9.4 Reach Park View Trail. Go left and down more awesome tread to Buck Gulch Trail.

10.0 Buck Gulch Trail. Retrace your route back to the parking area.

10.4 Back at the parking area.

Jeremy's Loop

Location: 48 miles west of Denver, near the hamlet of Buffalo Creek.

Distance: 15.5-mile loop.

Time: 1.5 to 3 hours.

Tread: 6.7 miles on doubletrack and 8.8 miles on singletrack.

Aerobic level: Mostly moderate, with several strenuous climbs.

Technical difficulty: 1 on doubletrack; 2 to 3+ on singletrack.

Hazards: Watch for car traffic on Forest Road 543 and narrow, sandy tread on Sandy Wash Trail 730.

Highlights: 8.8 miles of awesome singletrack with extended climbs and a fantastic downhill to finish the ride. The Buffalo Creek fire of 1996 changed the landscape and mountain bike trails in the Buffalo Creek area. This ride now starts from the Ranger Station's service building just off County Road 126.

Land status: Pike National Forest.

Maps: Pike National Forest; Trails Illustrated—Deckers/ Rampart Range.

Access: From Denver drive 25 miles south on U.S. Highway 285 to Pine Junction. Turn left on County Road 126

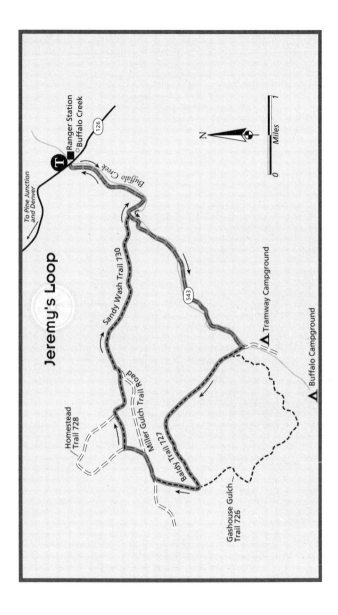

Jeremy's Loop

To Pine Junction and Denver

Ranger Station
○ Buffalo Creek
126
T

Buffalo Creek

Sandy Wash Trail 130

543

peol

Homestead
Trail 728

Miller Gulch Trail Road

Baldy Trail 727

Gashouse Gulch
Trail 726

▲ Tramway Campground

▲ Buffalo Campground

N

0   Miles   1

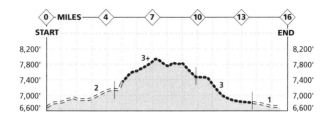

and drive 10 miles to Buffalo Creek. Turn left into the Ranger Station's service building's parking lot.

The Ride

0.0 From the Ranger Station cross County Road 126 to Forest Road 543. The mileage starts here. Pedal up Forest Road 543 along Buffalo Creek.

1.5 Pass Sandy Wash Trail 730 on the right. Remember this intersection. You will be coming out on Sandy Wash Trail at the end of the loop. Continue straight on Forest Road 543, climbing at a gentle grade past the Baldy Campground and over a one-lane bridge to Baldy/Gashouse Gulch Trail.

5.0 Go right on Baldy/Gashouse Gulch Trail.

5.2 Baldy/Gashouse Gulch Trail splits: Go right on Baldy Trail 727 and begin a prolonged and steady climb on excellent singletrack. The trail goes over a granite slickrock section. This is a great spot to stop and eat lunch.

7.2 Continue climbing, passing through a fence to the top of a ridge.

7.5 Roll gently downhill.

8.3 Turn right on Gashouse Gulch Trail 726 and drop into a fun singletrack downhill.

9.0 Go right on Miller Gulch Trail/Road.

9.2 Turn left on Homestead Trail 728, then watch for Charlie's Cutoff on the right.

9.3 Pedal right on Charlie's Cutoff, rolling over some rocky sections and down a tight, twisting singletrack.

10.6 Turn right on Homestead Trail and splash through a small creek. Thread through tight singletrack.

10.9 Veer left onto Sandy Wash Trail 730. Pedal through a small creek, then up a short but steep hill. Descend on tight singletrack, which leads to a downhill run sure to produce big-stupid-grin syndrome.

13.9 Reach Forest Road 543. Go left on Forest Road 543 to the County Road 126.

15.5 Cross over County Road 126 to the Ranger Station and the end of the ride.

Chair Rocks

Location: Buffalo Creek.

Distance: 12.6 miles out and back.

Time: 1.5 to 2.5 hours.

Tread: 3.4 miles on doubletrack and 9.2 miles on singletrack.

Aerobic level: Easy to moderate.

Technical difficulty: 2 to 3.

Hazards: Hikers and other mountain cyclists.

Highlights: A nice ride along a section of Colorado Trail to Chair Rocks and an overlook of the South Platte area. Much of the riding is through a burn area left by the Buffalo Creek fire of 1996. The fire consumed over 12,000 acres of prime forest and several homes. Later that year the area was hit by flash floods, made worse by lack of undercover destroyed by the fire. The surrounding area is just beginning to rebound from these events.

Land status: Pike National Forest.

Map: Trails Illustrated—Deckers/Rampart Range #135.

Access: From Denver travel south on U.S. Highway 285 to Pine Junction. Turn left and go south on County Road 126 for 13.2 miles to Forest Road 550. Turn right on Forest Road 550 and travel for 0.1 mile to a large parking area (fee area) and the start of the ride.

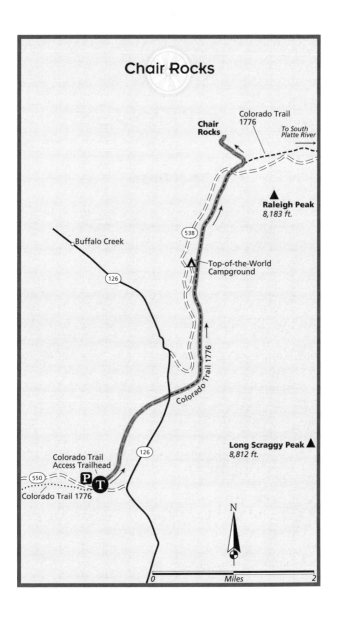

Chair Rocks

Chair Rocks

Colorado Trail 1776

To South Platte River

Raleigh Peak
8,183 ft.

Buffalo Creek

126

538

Top-of-the-World
Campground

Colorado Trail 1776

126

Long Scraggy Peak
8,812 ft.

Colorado Trail
Access Trailhead

P T

550

Colorado Trail 1776

N

0   *Miles*   2

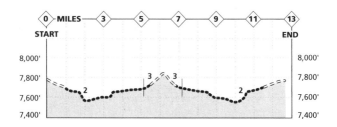

The Ride

0.0 From the parking area go right past the bathrooms on the marked Colorado Trail. Follow the wide sandy doubletrack trail down to the old parking area.

1.0 Go right at the old parking area through a gate and across County Road 126 to a trail along a fence line. Follow the trail to a gate on the right.

1.4 Go right through the gate and follow the slightly downhill singletrack through the burn area. The trail parallels Forest Road 538 to the left. Reach an open area and enjoy great views to the east of rugged and rocky Long Scraggy and Raleigh Peaks.

3.8 Steep downhill. Climb at a moderate grade up to Forest Road 538.

5.6 Reach Forest Road 538. Colorado Trail goes right. You go left on Forest Road 538 to an abandoned road on the right at a fence line.

5.7 Go right over the fence and climb up the old road past several humps to Chair Rocks.

6.3 Reach Chair Rocks and enjoy open views in all directions. Turn around and retrace your route back to the trailhead.

12.6 Back at the trailhead.

Colorado Trail/ Lunar Loop

Location: 50 miles southwest of Denver, near the town of Buffalo Creek.

Distance: 11.7-mile loop.

Time: 1.5 to 2.5 hours.

Tread: 0.3 miles on doubletrack and 11.4 miles on single-track.

Aerobic level: Mostly moderate, with several extended climbs.

Technical difficulty: 1 on doubletrack; 2 to 3 on single-track.

Hazards: Watch for tight turns; heavy bike traffic on weekends.

Highlights: Another one of those great Buffalo Creek singletrack rides. Bizarre pedaling through recent forest fire burns.

Land status: Pike National Forest.

Maps: Pike National Forest; Trails Illustrated—Deckers/ Rampart Range.

Access: From Denver drive about 25 miles south on U.S. Highway 285 to Pine Junction. Turn left on County Road 126 and drive 13.2 miles south, through Buffalo Creek, to

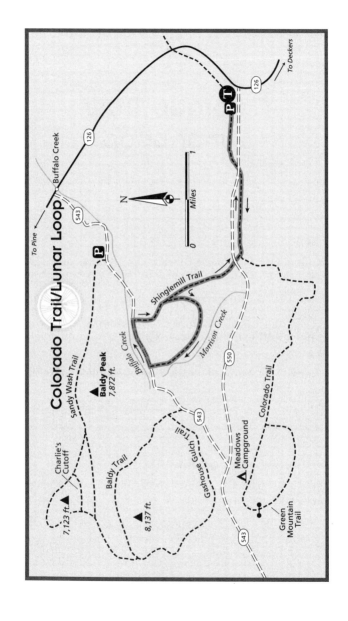

Colorado Trail/Lunar Loop

To Deckers

126

P **T**

126

Buffalo Creek

543

To Pine

N

0 — Miles — 1

P

Shinglemill Trail

Buffalo Creek

Morrison Creek

▲ Baldy Peak
7,872 ft.

550

Sandy Wash Trail

Charlie's
Cutoff

▲ 7,123 ft.

Baldy Trail

▲ 8,137 ft.

Gashouse Gulch Trail

543

▲ Meadows
Campground

Colorado Trail

543

Green
Mountain
Trail

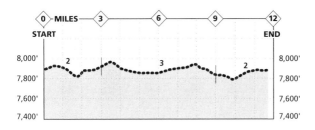

the top of a long hill and Forest Road 550. Turn right on Forest Road 550. Park in the Colorado trailhead parking lot on the right.

The Ride

0.0 From the Colorado trailhead parking lot, go left on the marked Colorado Trail .

0.6 Cross Forest Road 550 and continue on singletrack. Cross a small stream, then climb a short hill.

2.0 Pedal right on Shinglemill Trail.

2.2 Cross Forest Road 550 once again and stay on the Shinglemill Trail. Begin winding uphill on tight singletrack, through a weird burned area.

3.6 Go left on Morrison Creek Trail, which cuts between two large pines. Roll downhill on what used to be great hardpack tread. A recent flood washed out parts of the trail, leaving thick pea gravel in some sections.

5.6 Turn right onto Buffalo Creek Road.

5.9 Go right on Shinglemill Trail and begin a gradual uphill through a burn on tight singletrack. Scramble through a major wash-out.

8.1 Morrison Creek Trail goes right. Instead, pedal straight on Shinglemill Trail, up tight singletrack.

9.6 Cross Forest Road 550 and pedal up a short hill on tight singletrack.

9.7 Go left on Colorado Trail and retrace your route back to the trailhead.

11.7 Trailhead parking.

Colorado Trail/ Green Mountain Trail

Location: 50 miles southwest of Denver, near Buffalo Creek.

Distance: 17.5 miles out and back, with a loop at the far end.

Time: 2 to 4 hours.

Tread: 0.2 mile on doubletrack and 17.3 miles on singletrack.

Aerobic level: Mostly moderate, with several extended climbs.

Technical difficulty: 1 on doubletrack; 2 to 3 on singletrack.

Hazards: Expect tight turns; heavy bike traffic on weekends.

Highlights: Singletrack, singletrack, and more singletrack! One of the best rides in the Front Range. Don't miss this one!

Colorado Trail/Green Mountain Trail

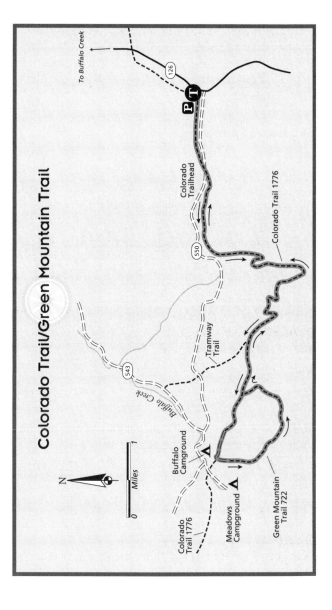

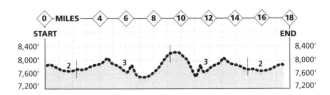

Land status: Pike National Forest.

Maps: Pike National Forest; Trails Illustrated—Deckers/Rampart Range.

Access: From Denver drive 25 miles south on U.S. Highway 285 to Pine Junction. Turn left on County Road 126 and drive 13.2 miles south, through Buffalo Creek, to the top of a long hill and Forest Road 550. Go right on Forest Road 550 and make a quick right to the trailhead and parking area.

The Ride

0.0 From the parking area travel past the bathrooms and access Colorado Trail. The mileage starts here. Go left on Colorado Trail and enjoy tight singletrack riding through the pines down to Forest Road 550

0.6 Cross Forest Road 550 and continue on singletrack, which soon crosses a small stream.

2.0 Shinglemill Trail goes right. Stay left on Colorado Trail, down a fun hill to an old, abandoned forest road.

3.1 Cross the road to Colorado Trail and climb a short hill. Then drop to a creek crossing and begin a long climb to a ridge.

4.8 From the top of the ridge, begin a long, fabulous downhill on winding, tight singletrack.

5.7 Junction with Tramway Trail. Go left on Colorado Trail and continue cruising downhill.

6.4 Green Mountain Trail 722 goes left; instead, veer right on Colorado Trail.

7.7 Trail junction. This time go left on the doubletrack Green Mountain Trail, past Meadows Campground on the right.

7.8 Go left to stay on Green Mountain Trail (now singletrack) and begin an extended climb up narrow tread over water bars, to the top of a ridge.

9.1 From the ridgetop begin a long downhill on tight, winding singletrack.

11.1 Rejoin Colorado Trail at mile 6.4 above. Return via Colorado Trail to the trailhead.

17.5 Pedal past the gate to the parking lot.

43

Meadows Campground to Waterton Canyon

Location: Buffalo Creek.

Distance: 35.8 miles point to point.

Time: 4.5 to 6.5 hours.

Tread: 28.6 miles on singletrack and 7.2-miles on double-track.

Aerobic level: Strenuous due to the high mileage. Be in shape for this one.

Technical difficulty: 3+.

Hazards: There are some road crossings, so be on the look-out for car traffic and other trail users.

Highlights: This is one of the best singletrack excursions in Colorado, favoring the singletrack and downhill cyclist. The only drawback is that you have to shuttle cars or have someone drop you off at Meadows Campground and pick you up at Waterton Canyon. Even with the hassle of car shuttling, this ride is worth all the trouble. For all you hill climbers, start the ride from the Waterton Canyon trailhead and head west, reversing the mileage. Colorado Trail is well marked and you should have no problem staying on track.

Maps: Trails Illustrated—Tarryall Mountains/Lost Creek Wilderness 105/Deckers/Rampart Range 135.

Land status: Pike National Forest.

Meadows Campground to Waterton Canyon (Part 1)

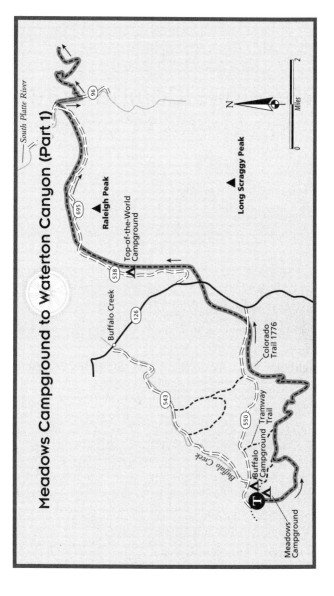

South Platte River

96

695 **Raleigh Peak**

Long Scraggy Peak

538 Top-of-the-World Campground

Buffalo Creek

126

543

Colorado Trail 1776

550

Tramway Trail

Buffalo Creek

Buffalo Campground

Meadows Campground

N

0   Miles   2

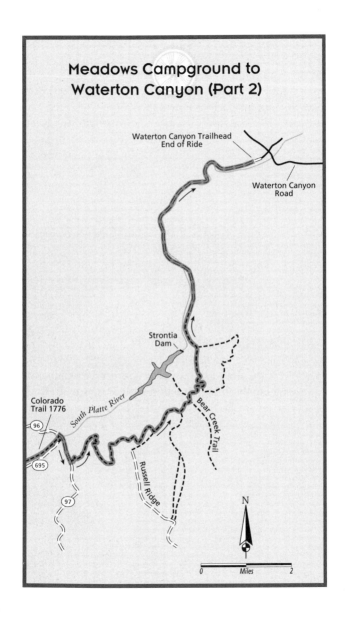

Meadows Campground to
Waterton Canyon (Part 2)

Waterton Canyon Trailhead
End of Ride

Waterton Canyon
Road

Strontia
Dam

Colorado
Trail 1776

96

South Platte River

695

97

Bear Creek Trail

Russell Ridge

N

0   Miles   2

Access:. From Denver drive 25 miles south on U.S. Highway 285 to Pine Junction. Turn left on County Road 126 and drive 13.2 miles south, through Buffalo Creek, to the top of a long hill and Forest Road 550. Go right on Forest Road 550 and follow it to Forest Road 543. Go left on Forest Road 543 for a short distance and turn left into Meadows Campground. The ride starts at the southern end of the campground, near a gate and Green Mountain Trail.

The Ride

0.0 From Meadows Campground head south past a gate and access Green Mountain Trail. Continue straight on Green Mountain Trail and begin a steady climb on tight singletrack through several nice meadows up to a ridge.

1.3 Reach the ridge and the end of the climb. Begin an incredible downhill run on tight, twisting singletrack (3) to Colorado Trail. This section of the trail is just all-out fun. Enjoy!

3.3 Reach Colorado Trail. Go right on Colorado Trail and climb up to a junction with Tramway Trail.

4.0 Tramway Trail goes left. You bear to the right on Colorado Trail and begin an extended climb on tight singletrack.

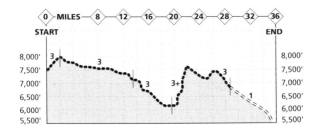

4.9 End of the climbing for now. Drop down and begin a fabulous downhill run to a creek crossing and then to an old forest road.

6.6 Cross the old forest road and climb up to Shinglemill Trail. Go right on Colorado Trail and drop down to Forest Road 550. Cross Forest Road 550 and follow Colorado Trail to a large parking area and bathrooms.

7.3 Reach the Colorado Trail trailhead and bathrooms. Take a short break, if needed. Still a lot of riding ahead. Continue on Colorado Trail, which soon turns to an old sandy doubletrack road.

8.3 Go right through the old parking area and through a gate to County Road 126.

8.4 Cross County Road 126 (use caution) and pick up Colorado Trail on the east side of the road. Follow the singletrack to the north, passing two paved roads.

9.4 Turn right on an eerie singletrack that cuts through an immense burn area. Continue straight on rolling terrain.

11.6 Pass a turnoff to Top-of-the-World Campground on the left. Continue on singletrack to a dirt road.

12.6 Cross the dirt road and access Colorado Trail on the other side. Climb up a short, steep hill and then enjoy a huge downhill to South Platte River. The downhill is somewhat loose due to the pea gravel, and the trail is side-cut in certain sections. Great riding the entire way (3), with good views down to South Platte River.

18.4 Reach a road and South Platte River. Go right on the road along the river to a bridge.

18.9 Go left on Colorado Trail and begin a long but moderate climb up to a saddle.

22.3 Reach the small saddle and travel down the tight singletrack to a trail junction.

24.3 Motorcycle Trail 692 on the left. Continue straight on Colorado Trail.

25.1 Unmarked junction. Continue straight.

25.6 Reach a trail junction. Follow Colorado Trail straight past the metal rails and begin a steep climb (3) on tight singletrack to a saddle and bench.

27.3 Reach the saddle and bench; a good spot to take a short break. Continue on tight singletrack passing a trail into Roxborough State Park on the right. Drop down on excellent singletrack, past a short (4-), technical section to Waterton Canyon Road.

28.8 Waterton Canyon Road. Go right on the gravel road and fly down along South Platte River to the Colorado trailhead.

35.8 Reach the trailhead and the end of the ride. What a fantastic ride and singletrack adventure!

Redskin Mountain Loop

Location: 50 miles west of Denver, in Pike National Forest.

Distance: 15.2-mile loop.

Time: 2.5 to 4 hours.

Tread: 8.7 miles on hardpack singletrack and 6.5 miles on dirt roads.

Aerobic level: Mostly moderate, with a long, strenuous climb back out to the trailhead.

Technical difficulty: 2 on dirt roads; 2 to 3 on singletrack, with one short section of 4.

Hazards: Light traffic on roads.

Highlights: Spectacular singletrack—when you die and go to mountain bike heaven, this ride will be up there. It follows user-friendly mountain bike trails and roads as it winds around the base of Redskin Mountain.

Land status: Pike National Forest.

Maps: Pike National Forest; Trails Illustrated—Tarryall Mountains.

Access: From Denver drive 40 miles south on U.S. Highway 285 to Bailey. At the bottom of a long hill turn, left on County Road 68 (Forest Road 543) and go 8 miles south. Look for a Colorado Trail parking lot on the right at the base of a short hill.

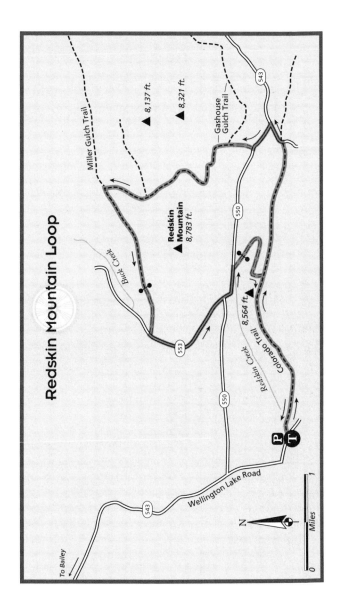

Redskin Mountain Loop

Miller Gulch Trail

8,137 ft.

8,321 ft.

Gashouse Gulch Trail

543

550

Bude Creek

Redskin Mountain
8,783 ft.

553

8,564 ft.

Redskin Creek

Colorado Trail

550

P T

543

Wellington Lake Road

To Bailey

N

Miles

0   1

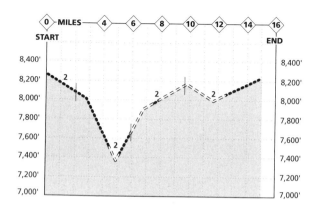

The Ride

0.0 From the parking lot pedal east across the road up a short, steep hill, then down to a small creek crossing. Continue on hardpack singletrack through dense pine forest.

2.6 Four-way junction with an old logging road. Remember this intersection—it comes up again at mile 12.4. Cross the road and continue descending on singletrack, looping through switchbacks. The trail then rolls along Buffalo Creek.

4.4 Turn left on Forest Road 543 and pedal west.

4.5 Turn left on Forest Road 550, cross a cattleguard, and begin climbing.

5.0 Turn right on the doubletrack Gashouse Gulch Trail and climb to a gate, where the trail turns to singletrack.

5.6 Continue straight on Gashouse Gulch Trail, through a burst of solid 4 moves, then up over rocks on tight singletrack. Climb through a clear-cut and onto doubletrack atop a hill. Bear right at the bottom of a hill, past Baldy Trail.

7.2 Continue straight on Gashouse Gulch Trail, which becomes singletrack again as it swoops down a short, sweet section.

7.8 Go left at a three-way intersection onto Miller Gulch Trail. Climb an old forest road to a closed gate.

9.3 Go straight through the gate, ignoring a road on the left.

9.8 Go left on Forest Road 553, descending quickly to where the road forks.

10.1 Bear left and downhill toward Buffalo Creek.

11.1 Junction with Forest Road 550. Continue straight, past a road on the right, to the second road with a closed gate.

11.5 Turn right on the second road, go through the closed gate, and climb steadily up this old logging road to the top of a small ridge and a junction with Colorado Trail. (If you start to go downhill, you've gone too far.)

12.4 Turn right on Colorado Trail. Weave and climb on this tight singletrack trail.

14.6 Cross a small creek, then climb a steep hill to a ridge. Drop down a short hill to the road.

15.2 Cross the road and pedal into the parking area.

Elk Meadow Loop

Location: 35 miles west of Denver, near Evergreen.

Distance: 5.4-mile loop.

Time: 45 minutes to 1.5 hours.

Tread: 0.6 mile on doubletrack and 4.8 miles on single-track.

Aerobic level: Easy to moderate.

Technical difficulty: 1 on doubletrack; 1 to 3 on single-track.

Hazards: Watch for other trail users and occasional water bars. This trail is a zoo on weekends.

Highlights: Excellent singletrack for the beginner. This is one of the more popular rides in the Front Range. Try to do this ride during the week when it is less crowded. Also see Ride 46.

Land status: Jefferson County Open Space.

Map: Jefferson County Open Space—Elk Meadow Park.

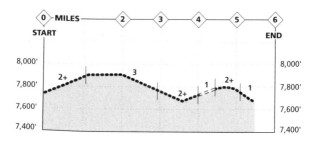

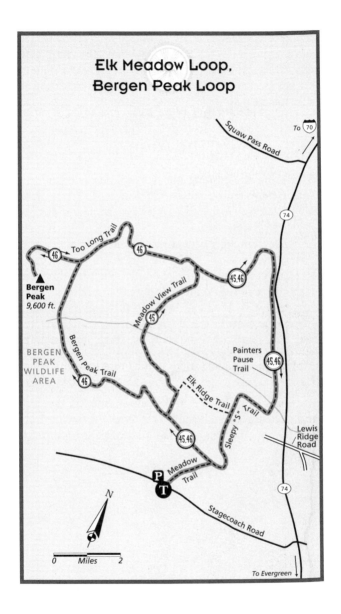

Elk Meadow Loop,
Bergen Peak Loop

To 70

Squaw Pass Road

74

Too Long Trail

46

46

45,46

Meadow View Trail

Bergen Peak
9,600 ft.

45

BERGEN
PEAK
WILDLIFE
AREA

Bergen Peak Trail

46

Painters
Pause
Trail

45,46

Elk Ridge Trail

Sleepy "S" Trail

Lewis
Ridge
Road

45,46

P
T

Meadow
Trail

74

N

Stagecoach Road

0   Miles   2

To Evergreen

Access: From the junction of I–25 and I–70 in Denver, drive 22 miles west on I–70 to Colorado Highway 74 (Evergreen Parkway). Drive 5 miles south on Colorado Highway 74 to Stagecoach Road, turn right, and go 1.3 miles to the trailhead and parking lot on the right.

The Ride

0.0   From the parking lot pick up Meadow Trail as it gently climbs to Sleepy "S" Trail.

0.3   Continue to climb on Meadow Trail as it turns to tight singletrack.

0.9   Junction with Bergen Peak Trail. Pedal straight on Meadow View Trail.

1.1   Junction with Elkridge Trail. Continue straight on the beautiful, rolling Meadow View Trail to a junction with Too Long Trail and turn right.

2.1   Begin a marvelous downhill on tight singletrack.

3.0   Junction with Painters Pause Trail. Turn right on Painters Pause Trail for a fast downhill on hardpack singletrack.

4.0   Go right on Sleepy "S" Trail, climbing over water bars to start. The trail mellows out and winds its way through a beautiful meadow to Meadow Trail.

5.1   Go left on Meadow Trail for a quick descent to the parking lot.

5.4   Cruise into the parking lot.

Bergen Peak Loop

Location: 35 miles west of Denver, near Evergreen. See map on page 165.

Distance: 11.3-mile loop.

Time: 1.5 to 3 hours.

Tread: 0.6 miles on doubletrack and 10.7 miles on single-track.

Aerobic level: Strenuous, with a long climb to the top of 9,600-foot Bergen Peak.

Technical difficulty: 1 to 2 on doubletrack; 2 to 4 on singletrack.

Hazards: Steep, tight switchbacks; water bars and steps on descent; a lot of trail traffic on weekends.

Highlights: Great singletrack, excellent uphill, and fast and fun downhill make this one of the better rides in the Denver area. Also see Ride 45.

Land status: Jefferson County Open Space.

Map: Jefferson County Open Space—Elk Meadow Park.

Access: From Denver drive 25 miles west on I–70 to Colorado Highway 74 (Evergreen Parkway). Drive 5 miles south on Colorado Highway 74 and turn right on Stagecoach Road. Continue 1.3 miles to the main parking lot on the right.

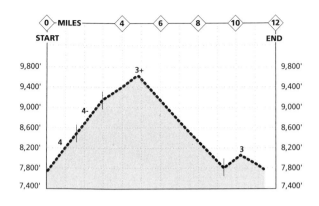

The Ride

0.0 From the parking lot pedal northeast on Meadow Trail.

0.3 The Sleepy "S" Trail goes right. You go left on Meadow Trail and climb gently.

0.9 Go left on Bergen Peak Trail, where the fun begins. The climb on this tight singletrack is strenuous and continuous. It also features steep, tight switchbacks that are difficult to ride clean, and level 4 water bars. Enjoy a short downhill as the trail drops to join Too Long Trail.

3.6 At the junction with Too Long Trail, go left on Bergen Peak Trail, grinding through a short, rocky section (a 4-). The trail continues to climb, passing an overlook with great views. Continue climbing through three more switchbacks, then enjoy a short downhill. One more short climb leads to the rocky summit of Bergen Peak. The views from the top make all that climbing worth it.

4.6 Turn around and descend quickly to Too Long Trail.

5.6 Go left on Too Long Trail, tucking into a long downhill on this great singletrack. Watch for water bars and steep steps. Keep your speed in check—a number of switchbacks are very tight. Also be ready to yield to other trail users.

8.0 Trail junction. Go left on Meadow Trail and roll downhill.

8.9 Go right on Painters Pause Trail, which continues the rolling downhill run.

9.9 Pedal left on Sleepy "S" Trail, over water bars and through a beautiful meadow. Grunt up a short hill.

11.0 Trail junction. Go left on Meadow Trail, down a short hill.

11.3 Cruise into the parking area.

Alderfer/
Three Sisters Loop

Location: 25 miles west of Denver, near Evergreen.

Distance: 7.6-mile loop.

Time: 1 to 2 hours.

Tread: 5.6 miles on singletrack; 2.0 miles on doubletrack.

Aerobic level: Easy to moderate, with a long steady climb to the top of Evergreen Mountain.

Technical difficulty: 1 to 3 on the wide singletrack; 4 on tight singletrack of Three Sisters Trail.

Hazards: Some tight switchbacks on the descents. Watch for other trail users.

Highlights: Great beginner to intermediate ride, with excellent views and wonderful, smooth singletrack for most of the ride.

Land status: Jefferson County Open Space.

Map: Jefferson County Open Space.

Access: From the junction of I–25 and I–70 in Denver, drive 25 miles west on I–70 to the Evergreen Parkway exit. Drive south on Evergreen Parkway to downtown Evergreen and a junction with Colorado Highway 73. Turn right on Colorado Highway 73, go 1 mile, and bear right on Buffalo Park Road. Drive 1.6 miles to the Alderfer/Three Sisters trailhead parking lot on the right.

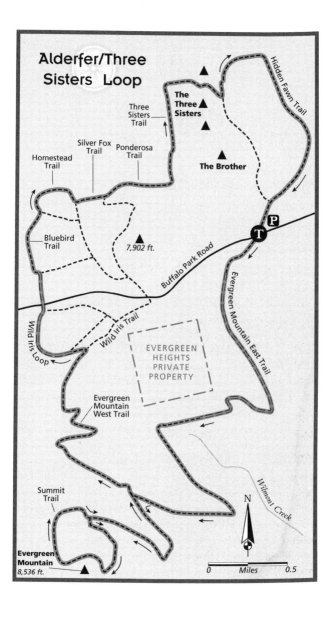

Alderfer/Three Sisters Loop

Hidden Fawn Trail

Three Sisters Trail

The Three Sisters

Silver Fox Trail

Ponderosa Trail

Homestead Trail

The Brother

Bluebird Trail

7,902 ft.

Buffalo Park Road

Wild Iris Trail

Wild Iris Loop

EVERGREEN HEIGHTS PRIVATE PROPERTY

Evergreen Mountain East Trail

Evergreen Mountain West Trail

Wilmont Creek

Summit Trail

N

Evergreen Mountain 8,536 ft.

0   Miles   0.5

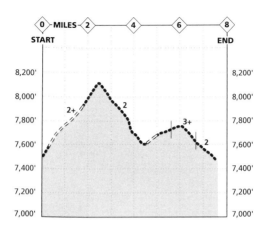

The Ride

0.0 From the parking lot cross Buffalo Park Road to Evergreen Mountain Trail. Pedal up this wide singletrack as it bends south.

0.2 Junction with Evergreen Mountain East Trail. Go left on this smooth doubletrack and begin a gradual climb up the eastern flank of Evergreen Mountain. The trail switchbacks uphill to an open area with excellent views.

1.8 Continue to pedal gently uphill through beautiful pine forest.

2.4 Trail junction. Go left on Summit Trail, past a scenic overlook, to a fork in the trail. Go left and loop around Evergreen Mountain.

3.8 Take Evergreen Mountain West Trail, dropping quickly through a series of switchbacks.

4.7 Pedal left onto Wild Iris Loop, crossing Buffalo Park Road to the west parking area.

5.0 Go left on Bluebird Trail, which soon bends north.

5.3	Go left on Homestead Trail and up a short, rocky hill to an open meadow.
5.6	Go left on Silver Fox Trail.
5.7	Go left on Ponderosa Trail.
6.1	Pedal left onto Three Sisters Trail. Here the trail becomes much more rocky (3+) as it climbs to a saddle between two of the Three Sisters' summits.
6.5	Continue down the rocky and technical Three Sisters Trail, over some steep steps (4).
6.8	Turn left on Hidden Fawn Trail and make a quick descent to the trailhead.
7.6	Close the loop back at your car.

Kenosha Pass South

Location: 50 miles southwest of Denver, at Kenosha Pass on U.S. Highway 285.

Distance: 13.0 miles out and back.

Time: 2 to 3 hours.

Tread: 0.8 mile on doubletrack and 12.2 miles on singletrack.

Aerobic level: Moderate, with a few strenuous hills. A high-elevation ride.

Technical difficulty: 1 to 3 on doubletrack; 2 to 4- on singletrack.

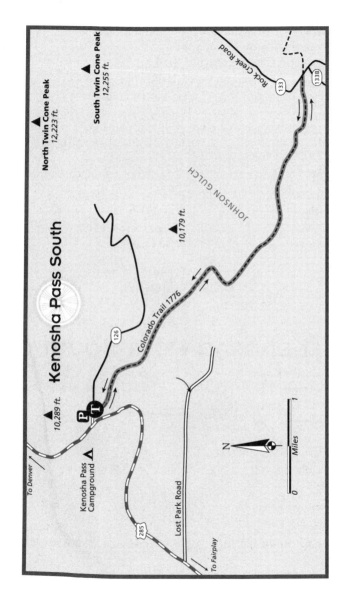

Kenosha Pass South

Hazards: Watch for other trail users. Several downhills invite speed despite rocky tread.

Highlights: Great singletrack; awesome views of South Park and the Mosquito Range. The downhill runs are an all-out scream. This section of Colorado Trail winds through beautiful aspen stands and a meadow filled with wildflowers. Great fall colors. Also see Ride 49.

Land status: Pike National Forest.

Map: Pike National Forest.

Access: From Denver drive 30 miles southwest on U.S. Highway 285 to Bailey. Continue 18.5 miles west on U.S. Highway 285 to Kenosha Pass. Turn left where a COLORADO TRAIL sign marks the trailhead and parking lot.

The Ride

0.0 From the trailhead sign pedal up the wide double-track trail.

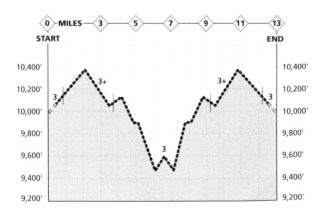

0.4 The trail dwindles to singletrack and winds through a beautiful stand of tall aspen. Gently climb to an open area with spectacular views of South Park.

1.8 Crank up a short but steep and rocky hill (3+) to a ridge.

2.1 Pedal on rocky tread to a steep, rocky (4-) descent.

2.7 At a COLORADO TRAIL sign go right and downhill on fun, tight singletrack.

3.5 Another COLORADO TRAIL sign. Begin a short climb up tight singletrack.

4.0 Top out on a small ridge and begin an awesome downhill on tight singletrack to a COLORADO TRAIL sign. Continue on singletrack through an aspen stand, where the trail opens up with splendid views of the Tarryall Mountains.

4.9 The downhill isn't over yet! Continue down on tight singletrack to a small creek and cross over the bridge.

5.9 Pedal up narrow singletrack.

6.5 Roll up to the Rock Creek trailhead and our turn-around point. Retrace your route back to Kenosha Pass.

13.0 Roll down to the Kenosha Pass trailhead and your car.

Kenosha Pass North

Location: 50 miles west of Denver, at Kenosha Pass on U.S. Highway 285.

Distance: 12.0 miles out and back.

Time: 2 to 3 hours.

Tread: 0.2 mile on gravel road and 11.8 miles on single-track.

Aerobic level: Moderate, with a few strenuous hills. A high-elevation ride.

Technical difficulty: 1 on gravel road; 2 to 3+ on single-track.

Hazards: Watch for horses and other trail users. Tight downhill runs invite speed, but ride in control.

Highlights: Great singletrack; awesome views of South Park and the Mosquito Range. Great fall colors; beautiful wildflowers in summer. One of the best rides in the Front Range. Also see Ride 48.

Land status: Pike National Forest.

Map: Pike National Forest.

Access: From Denver drive about 30 miles southwest on U.S. Highway 285 to Bailey. Continue 18.5 miles west on U.S. Highway 285 to Kenosha Pass. Turn right into the campground and park on the left.

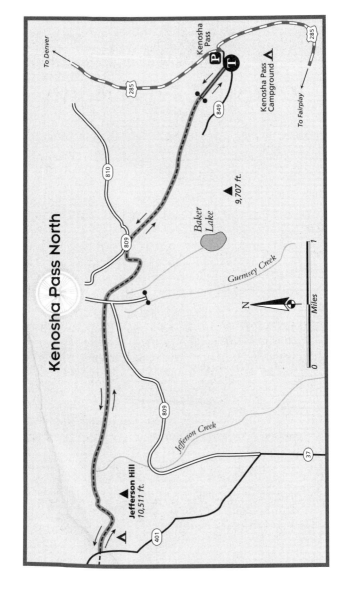

Kenosha Pass North

To Denver

285

810

809

Kenosha Pass

P

T

849

285

To Fairplay

Kenosha Pass Campground

9,707 ft.

Baker Lake

Guernsey Creek

809

N

0 — Miles — 1

Jefferson Creek

809

37

Jefferson Hill
10,511 ft.

401

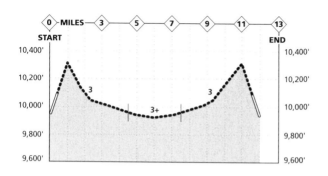

The Ride

0.0 Follow signs up the gravel road to Colorado Trail.

0.1 Turn right, just past a gate, onto Colorado Trail. Climb gently up singletrack, through dense pine forest. Soon the trail opens up with spectacular views of South Park.

0.9 Begin an awesome downhill on tight singletrack. Pedal through an open area to a tight switchback, then crank down to a meadow.

2.5 Pedal on singletrack to a small stream. Cross the stream and crank through a muddy section.

3.1 Cross over a bridge and pedal along more tight singletrack.

4.8 The trail forks. Go right up doubletrack, then bear left on singletrack. Bump over rocky tread and up a short hill.

5.3 Go through a gate, then down tight, rocky (3+) singletrack.

6.0 The trail dumps onto Forest Road 401. Turn around here and retrace your route back to Kenosha Pass.

12.0 Roll down to the campground and the trailhead.

Appendix

Information Sources

Arapaho National Forest
2995 Baseline Road
Boulder, CO 80302
(303) 444–6600

Pike National Forest
Pikes Peak Ranger District
601 S. Weber Street
Colorado Springs, CO
80903
(719) 636–1602

Roosevelt National Forest
2995 Baseline Road
Boulder, CO 80302
(303) 444–6600

Colorado Division of
Wildlife
6060 Broadway
Denver, CO 80216
(303) 297–1192

Jefferson County Open
Space
700 Jefferson County
Parkway
Suite 100
Golden, CO 80403
(303) 271–5925

Boulder County Open
Space
2045 13th Street
Boulder, CO 80302
(303) 441–3950

Boulder City Open Space
1300 Canyon Boulevard
Boulder, CO 80302
(303) 441–3239

Glossary

ATB: All-terrain bicycle; a.k.a. mountain bike, sprocket rocket, fat tire flyer.

ATV: All-terrain vehicle; in this book ATV refers to motorbikes and three- and four-wheelers designed for off-road use.

Bail: Getting off the bike, usually in a hurry, and whether or not you meant to. Often a last resort.

Bunny hop: Leaping up, while riding, and lifting both wheels off the ground to jump over an obstacle (or for sheer joy).

Clean: To ride without touching a foot (or other body part) to the ground; to ride a tough section successfully.

Contour: A line on a topographic map showing a continuous elevation level over uneven ground. Also used as a verb to indicate a fairly easy or moderate grade: "The trail contours around the west flank of the mountain before the final grunt to the top."

Dab: To put a foot or hand down (or hold onto or lean on a tree or other support) while riding. If you have to dab, then you haven't ridden that piece of trail **clean**.

Doubletrack: A trail, jeep road, ATV route, or other track with two distinct ribbons of **tread**, typically with grass growing in between. No matter which side you choose, the other rut always looks smoother.

Downfall: Trees that have fallen across the trail.

Endo: Lifting the rear wheel off the ground and riding (or abruptly, not riding) on the front wheel only. Also known, at various degrees of control and finality, as a nose wheelie, "going over the handlebars," and a face plant.

Fall line: The angle and direction of a slope; the **line** you follow when gravity is in control and you aren't.

Graded: When a gravel road is scraped level to smooth out the washboards and potholes, it has been graded. In this book, a road is listed as **graded** only if it is regularly maintained. Not all such roads are graded every year, however.

Granny gear: The lowest (easiest) gear, a combination of the smallest of the three chainrings on the bottom bracket spindle (where the pedals and crank arms attach to the bike's frame) and the largest cog on the rear cluster. Shift down to your granny gear for serious climbing.

Hammer: To ride hard; derived from how it feels afterward: "I'm hammered."

Hammerhead: Someone who actually enjoys feeling **hammered.** A Type A personality rider who goes hard and fast all the time.

Kelly hump: An abrupt mound of dirt across the road or trail. These are common on old logging roads and skidder tracks, placed there to block vehicle access. At high speeds, they become launching pads for bikes and inadvertent astronauts.

Line: The route (or trajectory) between or over obstacles or through turns. **Tread** or trail refers to the ground you're riding on; the **line** is the path you choose within the tread (and exists mostly in the eye of the beholder).

Off-the-seat: Moving your butt behind the bike seat and over the rear tire; used for control on extremely steep descents. This position increases braking power, helps prevent **endos,** and reduces skidding.

Portage: To carry the bike, usually up a steep hill, across unrideable obstacles or through a stream.

Quads: Thigh muscles (short for quadriceps); or maps in the USGS topographic series (short for quadrangles). Nice quads of either kind can help get you out of trouble in the backcountry.

Ratcheting: Also known as backpedaling; rotating the pedals backwards to avoid hitting them on rocks or other obstacles.

Sidehill: Where the trail crosses a slope. If the tread is narrow, keep your inside (uphill) pedal up to avoid hitting the ground. If the **tread** tilts downhill, you may have to use some body language to keep the bike plumb or vertical to avoid slipping out.

Singletrack: A trail, game run, or other track with only one ribbon of **tread**. But this is like defining an orgasm as a muscle cramp. Good singletrack is pure fun.

Spd: A type of pedal with a binding that accepts a special cleat on the soles of bike shoes. The cleat clicks in for more control and efficient pedaling, and out for safe landings (in theory).

Spur: A side road or trail that splits off from the main route.

Surf: Riding through loose gravel or sand, when the wheels sway from side to side. Also **heavy surf:** frequent and difficult obstacles.

Suspension: A bike with front suspension has a shock-absorbing fork or stem. Rear suspension absorbs shock between the rear wheel and frame. A bike with both is said to be fully suspended.

Switchbacks: When a trail goes up a steep slope, it zigzags or **switchbacks** across the **fall line** to ease the gradient of the climb. Well-designed switchbacks make a turn with at least an 8-foot radius and remain fairly level within the turn itself. These are rare, however, and cyclists often struggle to ride through sharply angled, sloping switchbacks.

Track stand: Balancing on a bike in one place, without rolling forward appreciably. Cock the front wheel to one side and bring that pedal up to the one or two o'clock position. Control your side-to-side balance by applying pressure on the pedals and brakes and changing the angle of the front wheel, as needed. It takes practice but really comes in handy at stoplights, on **switchbacks**, and when trying to free a foot before falling.

Tread: The riding surface, particularly regarding **single-track**.

Unimproved road: See doubletrack.

Water bar: A log, rock, or other barrier placed in the **tread** to divert water off the trail and prevent erosion. Peeled logs can be slippery and cause bad falls, especially when they angle sharply across the trail.

About the Author

A well-known rock climber with over 700 first ascents throughout the United States, and a mountain biker since 1982, Bob D'Antonio divides his time between his two favorite sports while living along Colorado's Front Range. Bob is the author of three rock climbing guides, four mountain bike guides, and multiple hiking guides within the Falcon series. He has explored most of the better trails in Colorado, often in the company of his wife of twenty-five years, Laurel, and his three wonderful children, Jeremy, Adam, and Rachael.